EQUINE GUIDED EDUCATION

Horses Healing Humans Healing Earth

By Ariana Strozzi Mazzucchi

ISBN-13: 978-1502377210

ISBN-10: 1502377217

*This book is dedicated to all of my students who
have become Equine Guided Educators
and to the horses who teach us how to be genuine, sincere,
sensitive, compassionate, and open minded. Remember
to follow the unknown as if it were a treasure.*

Table of Contents

Foreword

When Ariana Strozzi Mazzucchi asked me to write the foreword for her new book, *Equine Guided Education*, I was deeply honored and excited. I was honored because I deeply respect Ariana and the work she has developed: Equine Guided Education. I was excited to have an opportunity to talk about Ariana, her book, and her work. I first met Ariana many years ago at a somatics conference in Southern California. Later we published one of her horsemanship articles in *Somatics Magazine*, of which I am the editor. In 2005, at the recommendation of a friend, I attended the second EGE conference hosted by Ariana at SkyHorseEGE™ in, California. She opened the EGE conference with a stunning presentation that you can read in this book. Charismatic, she was a powerful and inspiring presence speaking her truth about the work with horses and nature.

Why did Ariana ask me to write this foreword? I am a licensed psychologist, emeritus faculty in psychology Sonoma State University, and I have been involved in the field of somatics since it's founding in 1976. I am editor of *Somatics Magazine*, and I developed a somatics approach for horses called Equine Hanna Somatics. After attending Ariana's EGE Level 1 training in 2010, I became a certified EGE practitioner and enjoy working with horses and people in that way. It is very powerful and effective work.

Ariana Strozzi Mazzucchi is a renaissance woman, full of energy, creativity, and a strong entrepreneurial drive. She is a zoologist, artist, poet, writer, gourmet cook, rancher (raising sheep, horses, and other animals), gardener, horsewoman, teacher, coach, mentor, philosopher, mother, and originator of Equine Guided Education. All these activities she makes available to others. She is very authentic. Her life purpose shines through her work. With all her intellect, she has a very big heart. She says that she developed relationships with other animals while growing up before she began to relate more seriously with human beings. She is still very connected with the world of nature. You can hear that in this book.

Equine Guided Education is an approach to working with humans with the horse as the guide and a human facilitator. EGE can be done with individuals or groups. Its purpose can be educational or therapeutic. "EGE encourages human growth, learning, and development through the eye of the horse," says Ariana. Horses are natural biofeedback systems. Because they are highly sensitive to environmental changes, they need to relate to other members of the herd, and they need to find appropriate leadership, they are very aware of the mind/body state of the other whether it is a horse, animal, or human. It is a survival necessity that they assess the situation and respond to it. Therefore, they wonderfully mirror the mind/body state of the client. Their mirroring is done non-verbally through their movements, respiration patterns, presence, and so forth. Their responses are relatively immediate given "horse time." The client and the facilitator interpret the horses' responses. It is the client's personal meaning and holistic responses that are the most important outcomes of the experience.

Ariana is a fountain of wisdom about the nature of the horse, herd dynamics, and horse-human interactions. In this book she shares much of her wisdom. For example, she shares with us the fact that the horse is a somatic and intuitive being. Being with the horse enables us to become more aware of our somatic, animal selves. Another insight that I appreciate has to do with the coherence of the horse. The horse's bodily systems are functioning in harmony, in coherence. The horse is very sensitive to the coherence of others. Living systems that are not coherent represent a threat to the horse. As the client relates to the horse the process encourages the client to become more coherent because the horse responds more to the person who is coherent.

It is energizing and inspiring to be around a horse. Part of that inspiration has to do with being in the energy field of the horse. As Ariana tells us the horse has a very large heart compared to ours. The heart's electrical activity creates an electromagnetic field around the horse's heart. The human standing in the horse's energy field is bathed in the electromagnetic field generated by the horse's heart. The client can be close to the horse when the client is coherent and pleasant for the horse to stand near. Therefore, it is very rewarding to the human to move toward coherence. Heart research shows that the state of coherence is a healthy state.

Ariana has trained many people in EGE since the mid 1990s. This book will give those interested in this approach a foundation of the principles and practices of EGE. Because it is written in Ariana's voice, the reader gets some of the flavor of the work. Ariana writes very honestly and clearly. It is very special. This book will be useful for people who are in the EGE field, those studying it, those who want to enter it, and persons working with horses in various capacities. The understanding of the horse that this work encourages is very valuable in a variety of horsemanship contexts. It will also be valuable for others working in somatics fields or other human endeavors because it presents the horse as a being with tendencies that are very human. We can learn so much about ourselves and our humanness in relating to horses in this way. Because Ariana fosters learning in a non-linear way, this book includes anecdotes/stories, poetry, quotes, and chapters by other authors. There is so much in this book: Every aspect of the book points toward continued exploration, learning, and experience.

Ariana is a master practitioner and teacher of EGE. *Equine Guided Education* is very informative and inspiring. In this book, she shares the EGE method to you and others who can make use of its information and insights because she feels it will be helpful to humans, animals, and the planet. It is a way back to nature.

Eleanor Criswell Hanna, Ed.D.

Introduction

Welcome to this new and exciting field of incorporating horses into human development, growth, and learning. I say *new* because we still have volumes to learn about the tremendous ramifications and potentialities that horses offer to human consciousness and healing.

Throughout the book I refer to this rapidly developing field as Equine Guided Education (EGE). If you call the equine-human relationship by another name, you can simply transpose that term where I reference EGE. The principles in this book are universal to all of the forms of this kind of work. In the early chapters I describe why I chose the term Equine Guided Education (EGE) and its early evolution.

I have been pioneering and developing EGE since the late 1980s and have watched the field develop into a new discourse in human growth and learning. I am a lifelong horsewoman, zoologist, and entrepreneur. I am thankful for the way the horses have taught me to blend my passions and help me to be who I am supposed to be totally and unapologetically. I have been teaching other professionals how to do EGE since the mid-1990s in addition to working with a wide variety of people including leaders, coaches, therapists, healers, shamans, equestrians, and youth. This book is intended as a resource for not only my students, but anyone who is interested or already practicing in the *horse as healer teacher* professions. In fact, the principles in this book are useful for anyone who is working in the healing arts, education in nature, and many of my students go on to incorporate EGE principles even when they are not going to be incorporating horses. As you will see in this book, horses are part of the process, but nature and her numerous other messengers play significant roles in health and healing.

I have been immensely moved, profoundly inspired, and overwhelmingly transformed in the presence of Equine Guided Education. I have participated in many self-development, leadership, and entrepreneurship programs and EGE trumps them all. In EGE, feedback is almost immediate, a person's willingness to accept the feedback is amazing, and the resulting integration of insights and learning is far more substantial than in anything else I have ever witnessed. My most profound epiphanies have always happened when I am in the presence of horses.

Whether we are learning about ourselves, experiencing life transitions, reconnecting to our passion, gaining confidence or finding our courage, horses tell us the truth about what's really happening in our interior landscape. They remind us to be intensely authentic and to have the courage to be truly alive. Horses are magical and mysterious, intuitive and sensate, serious and playful, rigorous and patient. I believe that EGE is the essential component that has been missing (since we took our education indoors) in our antiquated models of education and learning from pre-school to leadership training of seasoned professionals.

EGE also has various applications in the healing arts and is currently incorporated into coaching, therapy, cancer recovery, drug and alcohol rehabilitation, PTSD treatment, hospice care, and numerous other modalities.

My goal in this book is to provide an outline of the key ingredients that make EGE happen. While one cannot learn how to do EGE by reading a book about it, I hope this book helps you know what you need to know and serves as a continuing resource as you grow and develop as an EGE professional. The principles in this book are some of the principles we learn in detail in the SkyHorseEGE™ certification program.

I begin with several chapters on the history of EGE and its progression from horsemanship to equine-guided education. I share my deeper reflections on why many professionals, when they first make contact with me, say, "I feel called to horses" and what that means. The book progresses with chapters on the universal principles of the EGE process including reflections on the horse as the guide in EGE, the role of the facilitator, the various phases of the change process, self-development principles, facilitation skills and concepts, fear and judgment as inhibitors to change, non-linear somatic learning, and nature itself.

This book complements my other books, *Horse Sense for the Leader Within* and *Planning Your Business in the Horse as Healer/Teacher Professions* and my DVD on *Intuitive Horsemanship* by providing deeper and more specific topics regarding the actual process of EGE itself. *Horse Sense for the Leader Within* discusses the universal principles of EGE and the biological and instinctive similarities between horses and humans that make this work so profound. *Planning Your Business in the Horse as Healer/Teacher Professions* offers useful chapters on such topics as envisioning how you want to develop your EGE offer as well as facility, horse and financial considerations. *Intuitive Horsemanship* DVD shows some of the concepts of working energetically with horses from a horsemanship perspective.

Throughout the chapters in this book, I refer to both clients and participants. When an EGE professional is working with an individual, the term *client* seems appropriate. When referring to a group-learning environment, *participant* seems appropriate. Feel free to interchange these terms in a way that is most relevant to your particular pursuits.

The chapter, "Instinct," is written by Janet Crawford, a scientist and leadership development professional who attended an EGE leadership program in 2010. Janet is a pioneer in the application of neurobiology to leadership and corporate culture. I asked if she would write an article for EGE students on how the process works from a scientific perspective and she gracefully accepted. Neurobiology is a scientific lens that helps describe why EGE works from a scientific perspective. I remember many years ago realizing that while many professionals felt a need to ground this work in science, I did not need to do so because I had seen it in action so many thousands of time that I didn't need proof to know its profundity. And I am a scientist, so I do go by the *prove it to me* style of learning.

Two chapters in the latter part of the book are written by my most seasoned SkyHorseEGE™ instructors—Kansas Carradine and Hallie Bigliardi—who chose the topics they wanted to share for the developing EGE practitioner.

I am really enjoying being at a place now where I get to watch the seeds I have planted grow and blossom and create new flowers and new colors, yet all with a solid root system. I look forward to continuing to develop this body of work we call EGE, sharing it with people wherever, whenever, for the sake of healing our relations with ourselves, with our communities, and with our most sacred connection to our Great Mother.

Equine Guided Education

Horses are an ancient archetypal symbol in the human psyche, representing dignity, honor, beauty, strength, power, and endurance. For thousands of years, training one's horse was about creating a partnership of balance and oneness. Cowboys, Native Americans, Celtic warriors, and Spanish conquistadors truly relied on their horses. Throughout time, humans have loved horses and embraced them as family members.

Less than a hundred years ago, horses were our vehicles of transportation, agricultural support, physical laborers, and warfare partners. Yesterday we took great pride in training our horses for show and sport. Today, horses are our teachers and healers, helping us reconnect to what has heart and meaning in our lives and assisting us in re-aligning our mind, body, and spirit so that we can walk into our future with grace and integrity.

The unique ability of horses to listen to us and even speak to us in special private moments has been present since our relationship with them began. This kind of magic exists in the natural world as well. Trees, plants, animals, rocks, even weather patterns influence our sensations and imaginations. Regardless of where and when it all began, the new discourse of *horses as healers/teachers* as a professional endeavor started surfacing in the late 1980s and has become a viable form of human development and education.

Equine Guided Education (EGE) encourages human growth, learning, and development through the *eye of the horse*. Common terms such as the *magic of horses, horse sense*, and the *eye of the horse* depict the possibilities inherent in bringing humans and horses together. Why do these phrases naturally make sense? The word *magic,* meaning *to be able to alter one's consciousness at will,* explains one fundamental aspect inherent in Equine Guided Education and will be discussed in more detail later in the book.

Many people experience a sense of magic when around horses. This can simply be a feeling of lightness of being, or a sense of spiritual freedom: a place where there is no beginning and no end. Magic is an experience of possibility and synchronicity, where what wants to happen can happen. Anything is possible when magic is present.

Horse sense is easily equated with *common sense,* a once-natural trait that is being lost at an alarmingly accelerated rate since the invention of electricity, machinery, and automated transportation. People who live in cities and suburbs are bombarded by the electrical and mechanical pulses of their homes, offices, city streets, and outdoor environments. To use all of one's senses in such extremely over-stimulating environments can become overwhelming, which may contribute to the dramatic increase in attention deficit disorder, autism, etc.

Being in the presence of horses encourages our sensory awareness. We can access more than our sense of smell and sight when we are with horses. We expand our listening senses, our sense of being alive, of feeling our body – our animal experience. When we are in their presence, horses remind us that we do have intuitive and natural abilities to feel and respond to our environment. There is a sense of relief in knowing that we have an internal wisdom that needs no understanding. We can feel our connection to our environment and, with time and experience, learn a sense of cause and effect in our relations with others and with the environment.

When we are around horses we are usually in a more natural environment where there are fewer electrical and mechanical influences. These more natural environments are rich with smells and kinesthetic stimuli that further develop our common sense.

The *eye of the horse* represents the portal into our own inner landscape, a mirrored reflection of ourselves. This becomes a vital aspect of EGE because people feel seen by the horse. They sense that the horse is looking into them. They know the horse is listening to them. Looking into the eye of the horse is like having someone look into your own soul. There is a feeling of a friend found, a lover imagined. Feeling truly seen by the horse, participants in EGE often feel a sense of acceptance from the horse that they do not feel from other humans, evoking an increased willingness to be authentic and honest about their deeper feelings and desires.

And thus we arrive at Equine Guided Education, a process that is magical and profound, mysterious and transformational, and yet, despite its magic, EGE remains difficult to define. It's easy to say, "You have to see it to believe it." We are still searching for a more palatable, easier description than that to tell the story of Equine Guided Education and all of its inherent possibilities. There is more than meets the eye in EGE, which this book will help to define and clarify.

In its simplest form, EGE integrates equine interaction, kinesthetic experience, and cognitive reflection in various processes of self-development. A primary goal of EGE is the development of self-responsibility, a healthy self-image, and appropriate social and relationship skills. EGE can be found in a wide variety of human learning methods, including psychotherapy, coaching, holistic health practices, horsemanship, leadership, team building, shamanism, general education, programs for youth at risk, and rehabilitation programs.

The horse as the mirror to the soul is a unique component, as is the human's innate sense of connection to the horse and willingness to accept the horse's reflections. Even people who are afraid of horses will go the extra mile to learn from them. With horses present in coaching or therapy sessions, the client's core topics or issues can be identified in minutes as opposed to the average six-month time period it takes in our traditional talking models to uncover the deeper issues involved.

Horses help humans find their way back to their true nature as peaceful, relational beings. The ultimate goal of EGE is to live in peace and harmony not only with our human brothers but with our animal, plant, earth, and sky relations as well. And the ultimate, ultimate goal is to find our way back into re-alignment with our Great Mother and take a stand for living in a sustainable lifestyle that respects all creatures of the earth.

Before Equine Guided Education

Equine Guided Education has probably been around since horses first befriended man in early indigenous cultures. One only has to imagine a time when wild horses would graze near our villages, coming to join us at the fire or asking for extra treats. It must have been a natural moment when the first human (probably a child) decided to sit atop a resting horse. Many a time as a horse lies down resting beside me, I have experienced a natural urge to hop on, and as one, we rise on all four feet and ride off together.

Any seasoned horse person has a story to tell of a time when a horse spoke to him or her, a time when the person shared troubles, fears, dreams, and the horse magically responded as if it knew exactly what the person was talking about. Until recently, many of these stories were kept close to the heart, shared only when someone else was deemed crazy enough to believe in such strange magic.

All the best horsemen I have ever met have a story of one horse that changed their lives, one horse that forced them to let go of all they thought they knew and taught them how to listen with new senses, none of which are taught in school. In this intangible world, EGE begins: a horse changing a human for the better, opening her mind, helping her to see that all of who she is and who she wants to be is possible. All she has to do is allow herself to be open to new perspectives and possibilities.

The horse asks us to be complete within ourselves, to shine our star, to honor our birthright, and be the unique self we are born to be. The horse asks us to be courageous, to be brave, to risk letting go of what we *know* for what we can imagine. The horse reminds us when we forget, pushes us when we are scared, insists when we want to give up. And we, humans, will rise to the occasion if a horse asks us to.

Predecessors of EGE found a way to tell the story of the magic ability of horses to communicate to people what other humans cannot. Black Beauty, who speaks in her own book and movie (as do all the other horses in the story), transcends her own story as a horse and becomes a representation of the universal dichotomy between relationships built on love and those built on force and intimidation. Any human can find herself in Black Beauty's story.

The black-and-white television sitcom of the 1960s, *Mister Ed*, was about a talking horse. Mr. Ed was played by a Saddlebred and Arabian palomino gelding. His owner, Wilbur, had his office next to Mr. Ed's stall and so Mr. Ed would stand around listening to Wilbur's woes and dilemmas and then offer his advice. It seemed perfectly normal that Mr. Ed spoke to Wilbur and that Wilbur listened to him. At least, it seemed normal to me. I wanted to grow up and have an office just like Wilbur's. Interestingly enough, this TV show appealed to the masses, not just horse people. Why? Why was it not thrown out as a crazy concept before it ever hit the screen? I can only think that it is because people do have private conversations with animals and nature. And I don't think they often register this phenomenon in their cognitive landscapes. It just happens. Intuitively, it makes sense.

The predecessor to Mr. Ed was the talking mule, Francis, who was featured in seven movie comedies in the 1950s. Francis would usually only talk to his owner, Peter Stirling, which made for quite a dynamic comedy in both military and civilian life. So, I guess one can say I grew up watching EGE on TV even though it wasn't recognized yet.

My favorite childhood classic novels told stories of how a human who listened like a horse ultimately saved a horse that everyone else had given up on and the two healed each other. These books include *Black Stallion, My Friend Flicka, Misty of Chincoteague,* and *Call of the Wind.* Each story had the universal themes of love, redemption, and acceptance, which any human longs for. These stories that many of us grew up with were like sign posts stating the obvious metaphor of the transformation possible when in the presence of horses.

Tom Dorrance (1910-2003) published the groundbreaking book *True Unity* in 1987, speaking openly about the mind/body and the spirit of the horse. He also brought forward the important EGE concept that the horse mirrors the human, especially the inside or spirit part of the human. Dorrance grew up with horses and was considered a quiet man. He not only inspired the revolution in natural horsemanship, he opened the doors to the concept that working with horses was ultimately about working on the self. His words only hint at the vast ramifications of his philosophy:

> *There is so much variation in the human individual that the approach has to be a little different in order to fit each person. They might come out with the same results as someone else, but if everyone tried to take the same approach, there wouldn't be too many of them coming out with the same solution. That's another thing I think is important to emphasize – this is an individual process. I tell people that over and over when they are trying to get something worked out. I say, "All I can do is try to help." It has to come right out of the inside of the individual. There is no other way I know of that they can get it. People tend to say, "That's a little deep, I know what you are saying but I don't understand it" . . .*
>
> *The part that has meant the most to the horse and me is the communication between us. This is the part where I really had to devote a lot of thought. I have watched horses when they are loose by themselves or loose in a group; gentle raised or wild range raised, their naturalness will show. And by studying their actions and reactions I have been helped to understand how to present myself in such a way that the horses will respond to what I may ask of them. This I believe is true nature. This is something I had to develop in myself, for myself, by myself. The True Unity and Willing Communication between the horse and me is not something that can be handed to someone, it has to be learned, it has to come from the inside of a person and inside of the horse. Mind, body, and spirit.*

In his later years he shrank away from the spotlight because he did not like the commercialization of horsemanship that began to occur in the horse world in the early 1990s, fostered by some of his best students. Ray Hunt (1929-2009) was the pivotal character who brought the concepts of Natural Horsemanship to the foreground. He met Tom Dorrance in 1961 and studied his philosophy until it became his own. He wrote the book, *Think Harmony with Horses: An In-depth Study of Horse/Man Relationship.*

Ray Hunt resisted quantifying or formulizing his approach because he felt it was about *feel*. Every action depended on the horse, the person, and the situation at the moment. I attended a horsemanship clinic with him in the late 1990s after I had already been doing EGE for many years. I was fascinated that his words of advice to students were so full of rich metaphor. He focused on humbling the human so the horse could hope for more respect. I remember his words ingrained in my mind, "Through the life of the body, through the legs to the feet." He said this over and over again for three days. I knew what he meant, but I wondered if others really understood what he was getting at.

Ray and Tom were ahead of their time. They were the visionaries and spokesmen who paved the way for horsemen to accept the horse as the mirror of our deeper intentions and spiritual selves. Their message transcended horsemanship and they are worthy men to study to this day.

The following is excerpted from an article in *Shambhala Sun*, a Buddhist publication, which followed Ray Hunt through one of his horsemanship clinics and explored the Buddhist roots of his work with horses, calling him a Cowboy Sage:

> *Hunt may not have agreed with that characterization, but there are some strong parallels between the way Hunt approached horse training and the way a Buddhist approaches life: giving, discipline, generosity, patience, compassion, skillful means, wisdom, harmony, that's what Ray has been teaching.*
>
> *At the heart of Ray's teaching are lessons about giving, discipline, awareness, compassion, stillness, concentration, and intelligence, the Buddhist paramitas spoken in a western dialect. But how did a rough-hewn cowboy learn these things? Ray answers: "It didn't come easy. I didn't just scrape off the top and there it was. I dug and dug and tore my hair out. But I owe it to the horse to work this hard, because I used to do things the true grit way. Not out of meanness. Just ignorance. I didn't know there was another way."*

Sally Swift created another opening towards self-awareness when working with horses. She wrote the groundbreaking book *Centered Riding* in 1985, focusing on practices for body balance and an inner awareness of horse and rider. The practices ultimately create the understanding that how a person is in her body and awareness directly impacts the horse and the horse-human interaction. It is interesting to note that she acquired her knowledge and appreciation of Centered Riding from learning Aikido from George Leonard.

I too was influenced by aikido and spent many years studying aikido from George and Richard Strozzi Heckler (my husband of 19 years). In fact, my horses used to hang out right outside of the aikido dojo that lived in an old wood barn that stuck out into the horse field. A sliding glass door opened into the pasture, where the horses often looked in and observe the activities.

Even before I heard of Sally's work, I had already realized that I had been doing the principles of aikido, such as centering and blending my chi, with horses my whole life. Aikido gave me a platform to begin to explore my ideas with humans and horses. I began incorporating horses into the coaching and self-development process in 1989 in programs called Leadership, Somatics and Horses™ and Somatic Horsemanship™ (which I later renamed to Leadership & Horses™ and Intuitive Horsemanship™).

I began to bring aikido and leadership students out to the horses to practice energy awareness, the principles of center and blending with another person's energy. What I had not expected is that every person, no matter their profession or intellect, would say with great surprise, "Oh my god, this is what is happening to me at work." Or "Oh my god, this is what is happening to me in my personal relationship." It was then that I realized that EGE was about a lot more than I had initially thought.

Linda Tellington Jones is another talented horsewoman who opened the door to the notion that working with horses is about a lot more than riding. Her pioneering work in the 1970s with TTeam has its roots in her philosophy that all beings, humans and animals alike, are a reflection of the Divine

Whole. Her Tellington TTouch Training method encourages healing and communication that furthers inter-species connection and honors the body, mind, and spirit of the animals and their people. Her techniques focus on touch, movement, and body language to affect behavior, performance, and health. Her work implicitly developed the notion that we can expand our consciousness through how we relate to animals.

While I had not heard of Linda or Tom or Sally before I began EGE, I know they influenced our collective unconscious, and any of their writings and videos continue to provide education and insight that is relevant to EGE. As you will learn in this book, EGE focuses on bringing the magic and healing of horses into our daily living. A person does not have to be a horseman or even be interested in horses to gain powerful reflections and learning from horses.

A year or two after I had started experimenting with EGE principles, Barbara Rector was working at Sierra Tucson and began seeing the ramifications of horses in the therapeutic process and began her Adventures in Awareness. Even before the internet, the collective unconscious was busy at work dreaming into reality a new role for horses besides beasts of burden.

In 1996, Monty Roberts came out with *The Man Who Listens to Horses*, bringing forward the concept of the horse whisperer. While his book was still focused on the art of horsemanship itself, his concepts started to catch the interest of the general public. The movie, *The Horse Whisperer*, opened the floodgates and suddenly it was much easier for me to describe my work to the general public and have them understand that I wasn't crazy.

I started writing the first edition of *Horse Sense for the Leader Within* in 1997, but I worried that it was too soon for people to recognize the opportunity on a larger public scale at that point. I wanted to write a book that would appeal to both equestrians and leaders. The McCormicks weren't so worried and came out with their book, *Horse Sense for the Human Heart*, in 1997, which made me feel relieved that I was not so crazy after all. Linda Kohanov, a gifted writer, brought her first major contribution to the field with her book, *The Tao of Equus*, published in 2001, and *Riding Between the Worlds*, published in 2003.

EAGALA and EFMHA started surfacing on a larger public scale around 1999, focusing on incorporating horses into therapy and treatment models. It was at that time that I started to ask the question, "What is the horse's role in the process of human learning and development?" To me, the horse does more than assist or facilitate the process; he/she is the process. And so I began gathering friends and colleagues together to discuss what this field is all about. People would write or call me and ask me to start an association that would include other professionals because they did not see themselves as mental health professionals.

Since I had developed a reputation in the coaching and leadership development realm, they saw me as the obvious initiator. Although I was a bit reluctant, the quest to define this body of work had begun.

Defining Equine Guided Education

One cannot enter this field without experiencing confusion about where to start. As of 2008, there were over forty acronyms being used to describe the various methods of incorporating horses into human growth and development. Many of the acronyms are spin-offs of the three original acronyms that first came to form in the pioneering years of the 1990s: EGE (Equine Guided Education), EAP (Equine Assisted Psychotherapy), and EFP (Equine Facilitated Psychotherapy). These three acronyms are the most widely recognized and have been around the longest. They can be sourced back to points of origin.

I write more extensively about this subject in my book, *Planning Your Business in the Horse as Healer/Teacher Professions,* in the chapter titled, "What to call what you do?"

Virtually all of the acronyms use one of the following four terms – *assisted, guided, experiential,* or *facilitated* – to describe the role of the horse in the process. The acronyms either use the term "horse" or "equine." When looking at the various definitions of what the horse actually does, the word *guide* is the best description because, in my opinion, the horse does more than assist or facilitate the process of learning. If the horse says, "Pay attention here," I can't imagine a situation in which we, as facilitators, would choose not to follow the horse's lead.

When we allow horses to *guide* us into a psycho-spiritual landscape, we are providing more than an equine experience like riding or learning about horsemanship. If and when we are ready, the horse even guides us into a mythical landscape far beyond words, into another realm of consciousness that is ancient and indigenous.

Persistently pursued by the next generation of educators to define and create standards for this work, I assembled several independent groups of equine and human educators to discuss a broader brushstroke for equine and human education. We researched the best terms to describe the respectful application of *horse as healer/teacher* to human growth and learning. We researched the definitions of the following words:

Guide: One who takes one into unknown or unexplored territory.

To educate: To develop or cultivate mentally or morally; synonyms include: to train, develop, prepare, school, cultivate, and civilize.

Educe: The drawing out of a person or thing something potential or latent.

Experiential: Derived from experience or the experience of existence.

Experience: The actual living through of an event; the state or extent of being engaged in a particular study or work; knowledge, skill, or technique resulting from a particular study or work; the sum total of the conscious events that compose an individual life as observed facts and events, in contrast with what is supplied by thought.

Experiential learning: According to the Association of Experiential Education (1995), experiential learning is learning through doing. It is a process through which individuals construct knowledge, acquire skills, and enhance values from direct experience. Experiential learning occurs when individuals engage in some activity, reflect upon the activity critically, derive some useful insight from the analysis, and incorporate the result through a change in understanding and/or behavior. Experiential learning is based on the assumption that all knowing must begin with the individual's relationship to the topic. Experiential learning is a philosophical orientation toward teaching and learning that values and encourages linkages between concrete, educational activities and abstract lessons to maximize learning. What experiential learning does best is to instill a sense of ownership over what is learned. It adds to the interest and involvement of the participants, but most importantly it contributes significantly to the transfer of learning. The ultimate result is that individuals accept responsibility for their own learning and behavior, rather that assigning that responsibility to someone else.

Learning: The acquisition of knowledge or skill through experience, practice, study, or by being taught.

Coach: A tutor; one who instructs or trains a performer.

Facilitate: To make easy or less difficult.

Assist: To give support, help, or aid.

I imagined a blank canvas and I imagined what the painting of *horses as healers/teachers* would look in 2050. I asked myself the question, "What if we could start from the beginning and find a name that would cover all of the different styles of this work?" I imagined a unified field where we would each use a simple term, "I am an Equine Guided Educator," just as all chiropractors simply state, "I am a chiropractor."

I later explored the term, Equine Interactive Professional (EIP), thinking it might be a more universal name for the already established disciplines of EGE, EAP and EFP. I decided to stick with EGE because it embraces so much more than EIP. It emphasizes the horse's actual role as the pivotal component rather than a prop in our professional endeavors.

After much deliberation and conversation, I felt settled that the term Equine Guided Education did indeed cover all of the aspects of the horse and human process. It even covers horsemanship. The term *education* seemed better than *learning* because it not only includes a wide variety of learning models including therapy and coaching, but it also includes the element of teaching. Its definition includes the principles and practices of developing the *self*. The word *guided* offers the best possible definition of what the horse actually does, whether we are doing therapy, coaching, or even teaching basic horsemanship. It also feels most respectful to the horse and gives the horse the more predominant role in the work. We, humans, merely translate (well or poorly) what the horse is mirroring in an EGE session. The horse is the crucial factor, the one who reflects the essential elements of spirit and inner-psyche dilemmas.

Furthermore, EGE stands for the respectful integration of horses into human learning and development. This is distinct from just adding horses to experiential learning programs. It is important for professionals moving forward in this field to remember that what ultimately makes this work unique and magical is that the horse is a sentient being who can offer his or her tremendous spirit, courage, and hope to those who are dis-enfranchised and looking for a way to re-integrate themselves back into their lives. Therefore, the respectful treatment of horses is essential to anyone who plans to incorporate horses into the learning process.

Equine Guided Education encompasses the following meanings of each word that makes up the acronym EGE:

> *Equine: A horse representing the ancient archetypes of strength, courage, dignity, power, honor, beauty, endurance, and resilience.*
>
> *Guided: Being taken into unknown or unexplored territory through the magical ability of horses, to a place where we can heal the past, re-imagine our future, and connect to our life purpose and share our natural wisdom.*
>
> *Education: Cultivation of mind and/or character through study or instruction, dealing with the principles and practice of teaching and learning. Includes educational, coaching, and therapeutic models that encourage effective relationship, communication, coordination, and social interaction skills for individuals and/or groups.*

The Call of the Horse

The *Call of the Horse* is an interesting phenomenon that I began to gain curiosity about in the early 2000's. My Equine Guided Programs began to be filled with people who would say, "I feel called by horses." Even people who were attending the programs for strictly their own leadership development would say, "I am not sure why I am here. I don't know anything about horses, but I have been dreaming about them. It is as though they are trying to tell me something." Others would say, "I used to ride as a child and now I feel a tremendous need to reconnect to horses and I am not sure why." This *Call of the Horse* has been increasing since the early 2000s. I started to ask the question, "Okay then, why are these people being called by horses and what are they being called to do?"

I noticed that the people *being called* came from all walks of life. No particular demographic in terms of type of career or lifestyle stood out as unique. I noticed that many of these people were intuitive, sensate types (even if they didn't identify themselves as such). The one's who weren't aware of their intuitive gifts were like bulls in a china shop, sensing but not trusting their feelings. Some would blurt out their insights, lacking social grace and thus offending others in the group. Others would be so beaten down by self-judgment they were often afraid and socially awkward with others. They felt different, not normal.

In some sense they made good candidates for becoming EGE facilitators because of their intuitive sensitivity. On the other hand, they needed to develop social skills. They needed to learn how to speak what they were sensing and feeling in a way that took care of other people's listening. They also needed to learn that sometimes what they were feeling might not actually be their feelings or emotions but might rather be sensations they were picking up from others in the local or non-local environment.

During SkyHorseEGE™ classes I would ask the horses, "Why are you calling the humans now?" What I heard each time was that the horses were the messengers of the other animals and the earth and that they had been selected to call humans because humans recognize them. Humans are inspired by horses and are compelled to listen to their messages. Hummingbirds, dragonflies, bees, and many other animals are also messengers, but often the human is not even aware of their presence or their message.

Horses are calling people, catching their attention and asking them to awaken. They are asking us to re-awaken our lost senses, our intuitive abilities and ancient connections. As more and more humans become awake, they will in turn awaken others. And through this awakening, humans will begin to ask the important questions of our time and may be able to look at our unsustainable lifestyle with new perspectives.

Hopefully, we will collectively recognize how out of balance humans are with the natural world. We will begin to feel a sense of responsibility to envision new paradigms in learning, in social interaction, and in what it means to live a good life. We will begin to challenge corporate manipulation and learn to de-link from its consumeristic intensity. We will begin to ask the most important question of our time, "What do we need to change in the way we think and the way we relate to the whole system, to the interconnectedness of living beings?" We will begin to see that each individual has the opportunity to change our corrupt abuse of the planet.

If one human awakens into this potentiality and becomes a visionary for change, he/she will, in turn, awaken others and a growing group of awakened individuals will begin to feel that we do have the power and capability to change our trajectory. Rather than feeling disempowered and hopeless about loss of plant and animal species, loss of natural habitats around the world, or global warming they will find the courage to take a stand and find alternatives to our current lack of regard.

The following keynote speeches for the Equine Guided Education Association's (EGEA) annual international conference reveal what I have been learning and hearing regarding this call to action. Please note that I put the Equine

Guided Education Association on the back burner after eight years because I wanted to focus primarily on my SkyHorseEGE™ students and developing the SkyHorseEGE™ principles. While running the association I spent an incredible amount of time politicking, which I found rather futile. That being said, the conferences were a great way for me to see firsthand all of the other pioneering members of the horse as teacher/healer discourse at that time.

2005, 1st International EGEA Conference

Keynote Speech By Ariana Strozzi Mazzucchi

Good morning! I am proud to stand before you today and welcome you to the first annual conference of the Equine Guided Education Association!

The fact that many of you have traveled from around the world to be here, a few of you even calling within the last twenty-four hours and flying in from Canada, confirms that there is a call to action that we are all responding to. A call that rides the mystical waves of all that we cannot see, but sense, like horses do. So, thank you for coming all this way to become a part of EGEA!

We are here to honor the horse as *guide*. I would like to take a few minutes and share memories of my first horse. Her name was Sumi. She was one of those horses you might find once in a lifetime. She put up with my attempts to refine her gaits in the art of dressage, She loved gymkhana, and jumping fast. She carried me from the hills of Pt. Reyes to the shores that lap the Golden Gate. We frolicked with the wildlife around us, in our own little world. She was small but mighty.

She fed me many slices of humble pie. And at the same time, she was my mother, my teacher, and my best friend. She nurtured me and held me accountable to the highest of standards through most of my life, from age nine to thirty-five. My intention to honor the horse as guide begins with her.

We grew up together at many different stables. At each stable everyone had a different opinion about how we should be . . . *their way was the only way*. Their tools were the only tools.

After a while, Sumi and I figured out what worked best for the two of us. We found our own way.

In college I worked hands-on with wildlife, zoo animals, cats and dogs, and birds of prey. They seemed to know me better than I knew myself. And they accepted me in a way I hadn't found in the human world. They were trusting, patient, and non-judgmental. They communicated without words.

I learned to listen like an animal. The animals in my life, the horses, hawks, eagles, owls, bobcats, turtles, lizards, parrots, foxes, raccoons, deer, taught me one of my greatest lessons: To find unity with another being you need to *feel your way, not know your way*. Wendell Berry said it beautifully in this poem: "It may be that when we no longer know what to do, we have come to our real work. And that when we no longer know which way to go, we have begun our real journey."

The intention of our first conference is to encourage this sense of open curiosity and imagination – sensing versus knowing – instilling a *freedom of spirit* that animals embody into this association.

We do not have all the answers, and perhaps that is a good thing. We do not need to rush. We need to listen to the unspoken, intangible aspects of this work in order to create an expansive foundation that future generations can grow into. Let us stay open to learning, to sharing ideas, to thinking together and to bringing forward the amazing possibilities that emerge in doing the work of Equine Guided Education.

Let us re-find the freedom we had as children to explore and experience the power of *not knowing*. The horses in our lives remind us to this day that if we remain open to our imagination, we can make anything happen. We are here to partner with the horse, to create an environment where people *can* become their destiny.

At the core of EGE is the belief that people can change for the better, can find peace and harmony within themselves, and can learn to have compassion and respect for all life. In the years that I have studied the horse and human relationship, I have learned that the horse sees deep into the human psyche in a profound and magical way that science and rational thought cannot describe. It is far easier for the human to receive

24

feedback from the horse than from another human being. And the horse can take us into our own interior landscape and help us re-find a non-judgmental heart and a sense of meaning and purpose.

Let us now share this anywhere and everywhere we can. Let's encourage others to believe in what they are discovering, to live in fascination, and not feel a need to have to *know* before taking new action.

In the early 1990s I wasn't sure other humans could understand the gold mine I had discovered. But I felt compelled to pursue it anyway. Over time and thanks to the movie, "The Horse Whisperer," the public started to warm up to the idea that horses could be more than beasts of burden.

By the late 1990s I was tired of feeling alone in this work. I started searching for others who saw the same possibilities that I did. By the end of the 1990s it was as if a wild fire had started. People began calling me from around the world asking me if there was a place for all of us to belong.

I would like to share with you a vision: Fifty years from now I see each of us walking down the street saying, "I am an Equine Guided Educator" and people will understand clearly what that means the way we understand the work of doctors and nurses.

In the traditional equine model we may be the leader of the direction and purpose to what we are doing together, but the horse is the leader of the psycho-spiritual realm. We have all had experiences where the horse was able to sense, long before we do, when we are not aligned in mind, body, and spirit. I think that all of us here have experienced this. And perhaps that is why we are here, to bring this forward, to share it with others.

Many of you have left high-paying jobs to become artists of life, healers of the planet. You have been moved by something powerful and bigger than you. *Ride that horse! Live that dream!* Remember that the seeds we plant today will extend beyond our lifetime.

Keynote Speech By Ariana Strozzi Mazzucchi

As I prepared for this annual conference I walked the land often. I asked the hills a question. I sat on the earth, felt the cool dirt heat my blood. I was looking for a feeling, a sensation, and then it came: "Aha, of course, the center. What do we all have in common?

"What has compelled each of us to travel great distances, whether physical, emotional or spiritual? What has compelled us to leave our homes, our families, and our horses, to arrive in a new landscape, an unknown horizon? To arrive here, today?"

The wind replied, "The horse."

"Thank you for reminding me," I replied.

My brow wrinkled with another question: "What is it about the horse? What has encouraged us to take risks to reach for a possibility?" And the red tail asked, "And to contribute what?"

The horse. The horse is wild. The horse embodies our dream to live boundlessly, without borders or fences; to ride into the wind, to feel life; to allow all of the colors of the rainbow to live beside each other and within us.

Horses remind us of our freedom *to choose, to dream, to reach, to feel.*

Horses teach us *intention, perseverance,* and *resilience,* inspiring us with their *dignity and pride.* They are thoughtful. They love being in the moment. They appreciate a quiet mind. They savor a job well done. And yet, they surprise us with their unabashed curiosity and willingness to try something new.

And when we least expect it, when we think we are really cool and have it all figured out, they take us on a wild ride. They throw us into the air and deflate our arrogance.

When we have lost our confidence, when we need a shoulder to cry on, they offer us their tremendous love. Their heart wraps around us, a feeling of total acceptance.

They fly in our dreams like spirits carrying messages from afar, sometimes leaving just a feeling, a smell, a desire. Sometimes the message comes from above. Sometimes it comes from below, ancient, connected to all things. Calling us out of the darkness.

Sometimes it's a message into the future. A destiny not yet defined, but felt between the breaths. Sometimes it's the woman holding the horse; sometimes it's the horse holding the woman. A union of mind, body, and spirit. One blending into the other. A feeling of harmony . . . not understood, but felt. A feeling hard to put into words or to share, but compelling our hungry heart to reach out, to hold and be held.

And so we have each arrived here today destined together. Hearing the call. Calling in love, compassion, and acceptance. As a greatly respected philosopher once said, "Love is respecting another as a legitimate other." William Faulkner said that love is loving people in spite of themselves. The horse gives us this love freely, without grudge or judgment.

It is our journey, our ultimate destiny, to find this beauty inside of ourselves, this place of love and appreciation for another. Easy to offer our four-legged friends and yet it is our final stretch, our ultimate contribution to offer this love and acceptance to each other as the horse has done for us so many times.

2007, 3rd International EGEA Conference

Keynote Speech By Ariana Strozzi Mazzucchi

We have all arrived here because we have been chosen by the Great Spirit to respond to the most important message of our time. Time is of the essence. Horses have been chosen as the messengers. We have been chosen as the ones who to translate the message! We begin this conference with open hearts, clear intention, and a commitment to feel deeply.

"Wake up!" the horses say. "There is a war upon us. The air we breathe, the water we drink is polluted. The human's excessive materialism is destroying the climate, melting our glaciers, changing the ocean's currents."

Over two-thirds of the food we buy is now genetically engineered. Eight years ago, scientists discovered that over half of the monarch caterpillars that ate leaves dusted with genetically engineered pollen died. Genes from modified crops jump to other species and cause bacteria to mutate.

My neighbor, who initiated the organic dairy business, can't find feed that is not contaminated with GMOs. Scientists are making terminator trees that won't flower. What will happen to the birds? We are killing wildlife – everywhere – by our ignorance. The media lies to us. And we forget every day. We get in our cars; we buy food packaged in plastic so it will stay pretty. We buy everything, because we can.

"Wake up!" the horses say. They urge us, ask us, nudge us. "Do not let the pain stop you," the horses whisper. "Do not allow your spirit to wither under the pressure. Do not lose hope!"

You were made for this time. You have been preparing for this awakening. Your spirit is strong. Share it!

Do not bewail the sad times, but rather walk forward one step at a time. Begin by finding our commonality. Reconnect to like-minded spirits. Imagine the imageless. Communicate the incommunicable. Understand the unknowable. Follow the mystery. Call in harmony, the resolution of conflict. Move beyond romantic notions of freedom or plight, step out of the darkness. We are here to take action.

Dream of new beginnings. Remember that all things are connected: What happens to the polar bears will happen to man. It's time to inspire our fellow man and woman to wake up! Our time is now! Ask yourself, "What can I do? What must I do?"

You've come here knowing in your heart that we need to join together to save this planet. Hear the call! Make a promise. Take action so that our grandchildren and their grandchildren can still ride horses!

2008, 4th International EGEA Conference

Keynote Speech By Ariana Strozzi Mazzucchi

Welcome to the 4th annual international Big Sky Horse conference! We come together for these three days to think big, expand our horizons, and allow diversity. Let us share our ideas and knowledge, refine our perspective, and re-inspire our passion.

Before each conference I ask the Great Spirit and my animal brothers and sisters if there is anything special they would like me to say on their behalf.

I ask the question, "How many of you feel called to this work?" How many of you know what that means?

We're being called to be with horses, and to do something with people and horses. Why?

Horses are messengers. Mind you, they are not the only messengers circling around us every day. Ravens, hummingbirds, seals, hawks, dragonflies, bees, butterflies, deer, rabbit also share the magical qualities that we so easily recognize in the horse. But it would be a bit difficult to do butterfly-guided education. Then people would really think we were crazy.

This year, the honeybee came forward and told me her story and asked that I share it with you. The honeybee, as you well know, is a pollinator. She is vital to our survival, to horses' survival, in fact to the survival of all two- and four-legged's. Without honeybee, we have no regeneration, no flowers, no plants, and no food. She is the pollinator of life. She is in trouble.

Honeybees around the world are responsible for over eighty percent of all pollination. In the US, bees are responsible for fifteen to thirty percent of the food consumers eat. But in the last fifty years the domesticated honeybee population – which farmers depend on for pollination – has declined by about fifty percent.

Last February, for example, there were not enough honeybees to pollinate the almond blossoms in California. In Britain, where bee diversity has fallen, wildflowers that require them for pollination have declined by seventy percent. As of 2004, some beehive operators have lost up to ninety percent of their hives.

So we've been called by horses to hear a message and then to spread that message. Mankind is out of balance, and we are the ones who have been chosen to tend to the shift in our paradigms. We are being asked to pollinate new ways of thinking and solving our dilemmas. I know this sounds like a huge task, but we can do it. We can and we have to. One person at a time, by sharing our horses we are helping others to wake up. To realize that they can shape their destiny, that they can change fate, they can create change.

Take the Big Sky Horse perspective and answer the question, "If indeed, all life is interrelated, and we are all part of a larger web of life, then what does your work with horses and people have to do with the big picture, why are you really being called to this work?"

2009, 5th International EGEA Conference

Keynote Speech By Ariana Strozzi Mazzucchi

Wherever I am, I always come back to the horse. The horse listens to my past, reflects me in the present, and carries me into the future. I share this quote from Susan Chernak McElroy as a way to open this conference.

"I envision a world where animals and people can coexist in some form of sustainable harmony and mutual respect. Besides holding good thoughts, I ask myself, "What else can I be doing to help usher in such a world?" Perhaps when a critical number of people live the vision of a new way of life, it becomes easier for everyone to take part in this new life. As animals serve as inspiring examples to us with their "tea ceremonies" of how to live harmoniously and with compassion, so we can live as examples to others – examples of kinship with animals and with all of creation. Living our lives courageously can be our best opportunity to inspire others toward transformation.

You are the future. You are part of the paradigm shift, asking people to wake up – to remember the interconnectedness of all things. Do what you love. Love what you do. Do it for free if you have to. Share EGE wherever you are, whenever you can. Trust the vision. Keep the beat.

Keynote Speech By Ariana Strozzi Mazzucchi

Equine Guided Education is a vital part of the paradigm shift in consciousness, how we relate, what we value, how we care, how we heal, how we feel, how we navigate these times.

> *Knowledge itself does not enrich us. It removes us from the mythic world in which we were once at home by right of birth. The more critical reason dominates, the more impoverished life becomes. - Carl Jung.*

> *It is by logic that we prove, but by intuition that we discover. - Henry Poincaré.*

What does it mean to know?
What new story do you want to tell?

> *It is time for those who have spent their lives examining what is outside to relax into a new milieu of discovery within. To relax the mind's need to understand, to relax the need to define. It is a time of awakening, but awakening is not just about enlightenment and more consciousness and more understanding. Awakening is presence with and within the deep resonance of our own unconscious. - Unknown author.*

The horse is our guide to the mysterious landscape of our own belonging---The guide to the magical world of our imagination, to the ancient knowing before words, to the timeless opportunity to love and be loved. Together, the horse and the human create a story of possibility. What new inquiry do we want to discover? What new world do we want to enter?

The horse guides us into the healing presence of the story that resides between the knowing words. Bringing forward the imagination of the senses, whispering clues, opening our senses, and breaking down barriers. Are you listening? What do you hear?

Keynote Speech By Ariana Strozzi Mazzucchi

The horse calls to us
Whinnying her words of wisdom
Telling us to listen

To listen deeply with our hearts
To the earth's pulse within us
Beside us.

The horse listens to our stories
Inspires us towards selfless acts of courage
To remember our relations, our responsibility
To earth's creations.

Her words of wisdom remind us
To walk softly upon her
To change our selfish ways.

What will it take for us to heed this call?
What will it take to surrender our brilliance?
To walk among our animal brothers and sisters
in humble respect?

Instead we rape and pillage the land.
Build towns and cities in deserts and places
not meant to live.
We blow up buildings to entertain ourselves in movie theatres.
We destroy forests and decimate whole colonies of living
species.

We drill for oil so that we can drive our cars wherever we want
to whenever we choose. And in less than one hundred years of
mass consumption we have become a species of fat, unhappy,
ungrateful animals who now have to wage war for more
territory, more oil, and ultimately for more consumption.

What happened to living simply?

What happened to drinking water from the tap?
What happened to raising our children on home-cooked meals?
What happened to the red-legged frog?

The horse calls to you now. She asks, "What are you going to
do to change our trajectory?"
"What do you stand for?"
"What are you going to change?"

Stepping Out of Horsemanship

Excerpted from "Planning Your Business in the Horse as Healer Professions"

If I were to say in a nutshell what I have learned from horses, it would be, "Horses make decisions based on how they *feel*, not on what they *think*." Like wild animals, they rely on their intuition – pre-cognitive, sensate feelings – when relating to humans, other animals, and their surroundings. When a horse person opens his or her mind to this concept, a whole new way with horses becomes possible. Think about how different our lives could be if we could learn to stop thinking so much about how we are doing and what other people think of us and trust that we already know what is going on without having to think so hard.

Horses listen and respond to what is happening on the *inside* of a person first. They can sense when a person is afraid, timid, angry, calm, balanced. They want to know if we really care about what we are asking of them, if we are inspired by the possibility of oneness. Their ability to sense *who we are behind our tools* is their primary source of communication. The various tools and techniques that exist in the horse world are secondary and tertiary forms of communication that often rely on conditioning the horse into a specific type of performance though subordination.

Every horse person has heard the phrase, "You need to be the leader of the horse." But what does this really mean? Does it mean to dominate, to control, to be the *boss*? In Intuitive Horsemanship™ I like to reframe the concept of being the leader of the horse to mean being the *guide* who sets the direction and purpose of what horse and rider are doing together and, in turn, the horse is the *guide* of the emotional-spiritual realm. This reframing of the horse-human roles allows the horse to be the sensate being that it is, always giving us feedback when we are effective and when we are not. I'm sure every horse person in the world has had her share of *humble pie* handed to her by a horse. The horse will always tell us when we are not aligned mentally, physically, spiritually. If we can learn to respect this mutual, reciprocal relationship with horses, we can find that harmony that we all seek.

Imagine the horsewoman who comes out to the barn after a hard day's work. She's still uptight from the stress of her day. Her face is pinched, her breath short, her jaw clenched. Her horse fidgets and tosses his head while tied. She grooms the horse faster, still not breathing. He fidgets more. After saddling her restless horse, she enters the arena only to have him wiggle and prance around her while she is trying to mount. She still doesn't notice that he is just mirroring her mood. She tightens her jaw more. "Damn horse," she whispers. He flares his nostrils. "I'm just reflecting how you are feeling," he whispers.

She is so frustrated she wants to scream, but then she remembers this new concept that she learned – her horse's attitude is a reflection of her attitude. She stops what she is doing, takes several deep breaths, relaxes her jaw, empties her mind by feeling her feet on the ground and the breeze on her face. After several minutes she feels centered again and she mounts her horse, who is now standing quietly beside her. She didn't need any tools or fancy techniques to quiet her horse; she just needed to quiet herself. She focused on how she was *feeling*, not on what she was *thinking*. She got out of her mind's agenda to ride the horse. She re-connected to her desire to meet the horse as a partner, not as dominator. Basically, she allowed herself to become a student of the horse. This shifting of perspective, from dominator to partner, allows a whole new world to open up not only in traditional horsemanship models, but also in the new field of Equine Guided Education.

Equine Guided Education takes this concept one step further by allowing the horse to do what it is already doing – listening to what is happening on the inside of a person. Stepping out of traditional horsemanship models in which the horse has to be controlled, the EGE process focuses on allowing the horse to reflect how persons are *being* in the world distinct from how they think they are being. The horse's sensate wisdom with its insistence on honest communication provides profound and unique insights into how the person is dealing with other areas of his or her personal and professional life.

36

Another gift that horses bring to human learning methods is their willingness of spirit, openhearted patience, and non-judgmental presence. The fact that horses do not judge us as *good* or *bad* people allows humans to break away from historic, cultural, and familial conclusions that are rife with moral undertones. In order to truly create a space for learning about the self – to re-discover who we are at our core; to reconnect to our spiritual values and beliefs about life, place and purpose; to follow our destiny; to find our calling; to heal what has been broken – a non-judgmental, inquisitive approach is necessary. Why? Because our judgments about *who we are* and *who we are not* (as told to us by other humans or self-created) inhibit significant learning, growth, and change. Many of these stories about the self are actually inaccurate, outdated, and largely unexamined or even unconscious. Horses help us uncover these self-limiting judgments and create new, more optimistic interpretations.

The horse in an EGE process has an uncanny ability to get through our conscious barriers and listen to our core longing or life force. In addition, people will accept the horse's insights and reflections in a way that they often will not or cannot hear from another human being. In effect, horses help to reveal core issues, our outdated patterns of thought and behavior, dramatically more quickly, more accurately, and more deeply than just talking therapy or coaching. The horse bypasses our intellectual games and goes right to the heart of the matter. Literally.

Shifting Paradigms

In order to allow the EGE process to unfold, it is vital that the facilitator willingly step out of the confines of horsemanship as we know it. In traditional horsemanship models (including natural horsemanship) the old paradigm that we are always the leader and the horse should always be the subordinate follower is largely irrelevant. The goal of the EGE process is to encourage self-exploration relevant to a person's real life situation in their personal and/or professional life. When we are doing EGE we are not training the participant in the art of horsemanship. We literally are trading roles with the horse. The horse is now the teacher, and we are the student.

Horses can teach us to learn new ways of being in relationships with ourselves, others, and our larger environment. I believe one of the reasons that EGE has become so important is that it requires respectful listening and honest dialogue, which are the key ingredients to living in harmony and in balance with the natural world.

The old paradigm of command and control, dominant and subordinate, master and beast is breaking down at all levels of our social systems, including our financial institutions, government institutions, and corporate systems. This outdated paradigm is still predominant in most horsemanship models. I'm not saying that all horsemen and horsewomen throughout time have treated horses in this old paradigm. What I am saying is that many of the current models of horsemanship being taught to horse people are still contaminated with this distorted concept of social interaction. The horse is still a slave to the human's wishes.

One of the reasons that horses are becoming messengers for people who want to reclaim their lives is that they can teach us how to change our perspective on social interaction, leadership, and coordination. We yearn to break away from dominant-subordinate relationships and learn to create mutually reciprocal relationships in our families, our love relationships, and our work relationships.

The current paradigm and structure of traditional horsemanship as we know it does not teach this. In fact, it teaches dominance, control, intimidation, and "Do as I say, when I say so." Therefore, in order to learn and understand the dramatic potentiality of EGE, people have to break out of their horsemanship mindset. They have to let go of rules like, "My horse is being bad and therefore I must reprimand it" and "If I ask my horse to do something, he better do it or else."

Ray Hunt was literally on his own hunt for this paradigm shift when he said, "The horse is never wrong. It is your fault." He was trying to help horse people see that the horse was indeed mirroring something in them and that it was not enough to punish the horse for not understanding or going along with the horseman's plan. He knew that the human was sending mixed cues and unspoken messages. He knew the mechanics of the body of the horse and the physical presentation of the horseman's body and that is where he tried to make a shift in how people relate to their horses.

The unfortunate thing about his teachings was that while he was attempting to shift our concept of blaming the horse for our problems, he had not yet crossed over the bridge of EGE to realize that he was still treating the human as a dumb animal who was at fault. He had not followed his own theory out of horsemanship and into humanship. He had not crossed the bridge of, "How does my relationship with my horse reflect my relationship with humans?" and "How can I learn to understand and relate to humans through my relationship with my horse?" He was in touch with the *horse as mirror* but he still blamed humans for how they treated horses, versus teaching humans how to not only treat horses better, but other people, too.

There is no time for blame or disappointment here; let's remember that each of us makes the contribution that is ours to make, and it will be our students and our clients who will expand upon the bricks of learning already set upon our path. New bricks will be made and set. We are on a journey of re-inventing what it means to be a human being and perhaps remembering how to be an animal. Inquire, explore, and imagine: These are the critical actions to create change in how we think, how we relate, and how we teach. There is a lot left to discover.

EGE requires that the horsewoman shift her perspective from *the horse is a tool for me to control* to *the horse is a sensate being who mirrors my deeper intention*s. In some cultures, there are two definitions of the word riding. One definition is, "Using a horse as a tool to get around." The other, far more interesting definition is, "Developing the self through one's relationship with one's horse."

When ready to realize that the horse's performance and attitude is a direct reflection of the rider's beliefs and intentions (even when buried in the subconscious), the horse person must take responsibility not only for himself or herself, but for the horse's attitude and performance. By denying that the horse's behavior is a reflection of one's own story, mood, and attitude, self-development is lost. And so is true horsemanship. In its place is a missed opportunity to take full responsibility for how our personal and professional relationships are turning out. It becomes easy and natural to blame the horse, the trainer, the other horse people at the barn, even the weather, for everything.

Taking responsibility for how our horse is responding is the same practice as taking responsibility for how our life is turning out in our current situation. This requires a certain amount of bravery and humility. This means letting go of our habits of controlling the horse and requiring it to submit or surrender its perspective. EGE requires that we listen to the horse's perspective and explore how the horse is mirroring our deeper intentions, fears, and beliefs.

I know from having worked with so many people that shifting from *horse as tool* to *horse as mirror* can be very difficult for seasoned horse people. I often say that horse people will be the last to understand or even be interested in EGE. Ten years ago, horse owners would come to me in private to express their fears and disappointments with how their horses were being treated at the barn by other equestrians and trainers. But they were too afraid to stand up to their trainers, to say they did not want to learn how to dominate the horse. It didn't feel right to them. But one by one, these brave people have taken a stand and now some horse trainers, instructors, and barn managers are starting to become curious about the possibilities that EGE can offer.

I also know that EGE challenges so much of what we know and what we have learned about how to train horses that some people are not ready for such a significant shift in their paradigm.

These horsemen, teaching traditional horsemanship in a natural way, began to articulate some of the universal principles behind *horse as healer/teacher,* but I don't think they took their wisdom out of the arena. By this, I mean that they did not step out of the horsemanship model to really relate the profoundness – the broader applications – of these concepts to human development. They may have seen and understood the *horse as healer/teacher*, but they chose to keep it within the horsemanship model.

Subsequent generations of horsemen and horsewomen expanded on these earlier teachings and began to explore how the practices they learned with their horses could apply to other areas of their life. Some of the principles of horsemanship maintain the same beliefs towards horses as EGE. These include:

- Observe, remember, and compare.

- The slower you do it, the quicker you find it.

- Feel what the horse is feeling.

- Do less and get more.

- The horse is never wrong.

Horsemanship Principles We Expand On

- Horsemanship is about self-development, not training horses. What is happening on the inside (spirit) of a person directly impacts the horse and is the first source of information and communication. It is not about tools/techniques, it is about what you believe in that moment.

Horsemanship Principles We Leave Behind

- In EGE we let go of the premise that the primary focus is on completing the activity. The success of an EGE exercise is not that we get the horse to actually complete a specific exercise; rather, the purpose of the exercise is to observe what the horse is reflecting about us and how that relates to our life in the human world.

- In EGE we let go of the notion that "the horse shouldn't be doing that, so correct the behavior, now." What the participant is learning is more important than making sure the horse is performing correctly. For example, if a horse is pushing on a person who is holding the horse with a halter and lead rope, (which in a horsemanship paradigm would be inappropriate), we reflect on why the horse is responding to the person in this way. At first, we do not emphasize correcting the horse's behavior. We may ask, "What is happening for you right now?" "What are you thinking about?" "Is this mirroring another situation in your life where you feel pushed around by someone?" Depending on what subject matter arises, we then work to correct the relationship between the horse and person. The horse is not wrong for pushing the person, the horse is simply mirroring something within the person that we want to learn more about.

- In EGE, we let go of the horsemanship rule, "If you asked the horse to do something, you *have* to make him do it." Sometimes the person is not ready to perform the exercise you facilitated and it is unfair to both the horse and person to continue with the exercise (especially since the focus is not on training the horse). In this paradigm shift, the horse seems to understand that the focus is more on the person and does not tend to think it is getting away with something, as we may fear.

- Of course, the nuances of the response of the horse to the person and the facilitator's expectations are not as easy to juggle as I make it sound. It takes skill, timing, deep listening, and experience to determine the numerous factors contributing to any given situation. The ability to know when you are practicing horsemanship or EGE takes practice, inquisitiveness, and a willingness to challenge our inherited concepts of how we should treat horses.

CHALLENGE YOUR KNOWINGNESS

Shifting paradigms requires you to let go of what you know about horsemanship. The line between horsemanship and EGE is fuzzy at best. Believe me, it took me a long time to experiment and explore where one ends and the other begins. In fact, I am still exploring it. I think it is important enough that I dedicated a whole chapter to it in which I am attempting to offer some tools or ways of exploring it for yourself.

During EGE, it is important to let go of fears that your horse will develop bad habits. Because we are not focusing on training the horse in EGE, the horse will sometimes do things that normally would be considered bad behavior.

Horsemanship Principles that Translate to Human Development

- I am responsible for myself and in so doing I contribute to the safety of the horse.

- I promise to own my inner emotional state – fear, excitement, frustration, boredom.

- I promise not to over-use my intellect when I work with my horse.

- I promise that I will not judge myself or my horse; we are just learning how to be better partners.

- I will listen to the horse's feedback about my energy and intentions.

44

- I promise to be trustworthy.

- I promise to be sincere.

- I promise to develop my ability to be reliable and consistent.

- I will focus on my mental, physical, and spiritual energy.

- I promise to be a clean slate.

- I take responsibility for my horse's mistakes.

- I commit to self-reflection.

- When the horse isn't doing what I want, it is a reflection of me.

- My goal is to create a win-win scenario between me and my horse.

- Every horse is unique, with his own quirks, assets, and limitations.

- If I don't believe the horse will follow me, he won't.

- The horse responds to what is inside of me.

- I commit to develop my feel, timing, and curiosity.

- I will allow creativity and imagination in a respectful way.

- I will treat the horse as I would want to be treated.

Horse as healer/teacher takes these concepts several steps further. What we have learned since the late 1980s is that a person can focus on personal or professional issues while interacting with horses (rather than focusing on horsemanship itself) and receive dramatic, unique, profound, and concise feedback that pertains to real life. Uncanny, magical, mysterious? Yes to all. Beyond Cartesian understanding? Yes. Yet the information gained is far more useful and impactful than that evoked through traditional talking therapy or coaching models.

(The following notes are excerpted from recordings of Ariana Strozzi Mazzucchi at an Intuitive Horsemanship™ workshop)

I think the traditional horsemanship fear is that when we are doing EGE we're going to let the horse get away with bad habits, and then we're going to ruin our horses. Yet, there is a way to do EGE and not lose our horses.

If we look at the traditional or historic horsemanship model, there are stylistic differences, but basically if you ask the horse to do something he's got to do it; the horse is expected to behave. He is expected to perform, be obedient, and not question your authority. A classic foundation in all horsemanship models is that the horse should never push into you or into your space.

In the development of a young horse, there is a time and place when the horse needs to learn to respect a person's boundaries. For example, when I'm walking a horse in hand, leading a horse down the breezeway, or I'm in a show, I want that horse to have a very clear boundary and to be following my direction. He's supposed to position himself in a specific place in relation to my physical presence. He's not supposed to be putting his head in my space, and he's not supposed to be pushing his shoulder into me. It's totally unacceptable. It's unacceptable because it's not safe and it means he is not respecting my authority. If I'm in a situation where I need to handle a fractious horse, I cannot afford for my safety or his safety to have him running through me. It's very important when training a horse that clear boundaries and respect for the human's space are established at an early age.

On the other hand, when we move into an EGE process, the focus of how the horse and human are relating together totally changes. In the EGE process the emphasis is not on training horses or teaching horsemanship. Rather, its focus is on the human's self-development process and how the horse as the mirror of the human's desires, stories, attitudes, and moods

46

can reveal important learning and change opportunities for the human.

When doing EGE professionally, a day will come when somebody walks into your barn with boundary issues, and the horse who has never had boundary issues is going to nip this person, push him or her around, or become overly aggressive. A horse trainer would say, "You can't let him do that." Now, a horse person and an EGE person could agree that it is not really okay for a horse to nip somebody. In the horsemanship mode, you would reprimand the horse for behavior like that. In EGE mode, you would be curious about why the horse reacted that way to that person at that specific moment. In EGE mode, if you rush to reprimand the horse, you are punishing him for doing EGE work and you lose the moment of opportunity to explore the underlying reflections that the horse is making.

It's a real dance between your horsemanship mode and EGE mode to know what to allow the horse to do and what not to allow the horse to do. You have to unlearn some of your rules about horsemanship. When you begin doing EGE work, this can be very uncomfortable because your history says it's not okay for the horse to misbehave. Horse trainers are afraid that if you let the horse do whatever it wants in an EGE process, then when you go back to leading your horse down the breezeway he will have lost his manners and formed bad habits. I have not found that to be the case.

Below are a few stories that illustrate the possibilities that become available when we step outside of horsemanship as we have known it historically.

FINDING HER VOICE

It was a warm fall afternoon when I first met Sheri. She had scheduled a riding lesson. The barn was full of distractions the day she arrived at the ranch. Stacy was grooming her bay mare near the tack room and Jane had just finished working her yearling filly. I busily readied Sadie with a saddle for Sheri to ride. As Sheri began to speak about herself, I realized that perhaps she had not come to ride after all. I suggested we sit in the tack room and get acquainted. She told me about her and her horse, Silver.

"What would you like to gain from our work together?" I asked.

"I don't know. I saw an article in the *Chronicle* about you and it just seemed right to schedule a session with you. I have a horse named Silver. He is an incredible horse! He has become a wonderful jumper and currently competes in eventing. I don't show him, but I have him with a trainer who works with him and shows him."

As she continued, she revealed that she was confused about what to do with her horse at the current barn where he was boarded. She lived in Marin and made the one-hour drive up to Sonoma twice a week to ride Silver. She began to get tears in her eyes as she confessed that she was afraid to ride him.

"I don't know why I am afraid. I have always been a good rider. I used to compete, myself. He is such a wonderful horse, I don't know if I should ride him anymore. But it is important for me to ride." More tears welled up in her eyes. "I don't know why I am so emotional about this. I just want Silver to be happy. He is such an amazing athlete he should be on the show circuit."

"Who said he should be showing?" I asked. It seemed that she had an unexamined notion that just because he was a great show horse he should be on the show circuit.

"Well, the trainer thinks it is important," she replied.

"What do you, Sheri, care about? What kind of relationship do you want to have with Silver?" I asked.

"Competing was such an important experience for me. It taught me about focus and being assertive. Usually I consider myself to be an assertive person. I don't understand why I am so confused now." She sighed. A few more tears later she continued, "I don't feel that confidence I used to feel. But I love to watch him be shown by this young gal at the ranch. And I really want to support the sport that I love so much that has done so much for me throughout my life. I love giving this young woman a chance to ride a great horse, but I think I have forgotten about me."

By the end of our first session, we got clear that she needed to think about what kind of riding she wanted to do now and if Silver was the best horse for her. We also uncluttered the notion that just because Silver was a great show horse, it didn't mean he had to be shown. This revealed her realization that she was still afraid of Silver, that perhaps he was too much horse for her. We also discussed that Silver was *her* horse and that it was her choice to decide whether to show him or not. Although the trainer wanted to show the horse, Sheri needed to make sure that she was taking care of herself and her relationship with Silver. She realized how powerless she felt in speaking her mind to her trainer.

During subsequent sessions, she was able to unravel old stories about power. Historically, she had gained a sense of power and accomplishment in showing. She was very dedicated to the sport of eventing and perhaps it was time to create a new story of how she could contribute to the sport and engage in it without being the one showing. She was redefining what it meant to be powerful and influential in the equestrian world. She also practiced taking a stand for what she cared about and being able to have conversations with the trainer about how she wanted her horse trained and shown as opposed to being submissive and feeling powerless.

This last notion was significant. Riders like Sheri give trainers so much authority that over time they begin to feel that they don't have a voice anymore. There is an unspoken agreement at many training stables that you do things the way the trainer says to without question. Of course, a show trainer wants a horse to be shown. It's how he makes his living. When Sheri listened quietly to Silver, she got the sense that he didn't care whether he showed or not, he really enjoyed his relationship with her. She decided that, rather than forcing herself and Silver back into the show ring, she would put her passion for showing into supporting younger riders and sponsoring local horse shows. In one EGE session, she practiced with Sadie standing up to the trainer and telling him that she had decided not to pursue a showing career for herself or Silver. Once she felt confident, she took a stand and was at once relieved by her decision.

She and Silver were able to experience a depth in their relationship that would have been missed if she had listened to the trainer and bought the show package. Silver flourished under her care. And she flourished under his.

ALABAMA, By Rick Coberly

As I stood in the round pen with tears welling in my eyes, only one question leapt forward from my body as I observed this magnificent horse. "What's your story?" I asked from the most compassionate place I could reach.

He stood quietly – even though his eyes were frightened and confused.

"How did things get this far?" I asked. "Are you the dangerous, out-of-control horse they say you are?"

"I don't know how this happened. Everything happened so fast. They hurt me, then sent me away. The train was terrifying and it was difficult to stand with my injury. I had no idea where I was going or why they sent me away – nobody told me anything. I have been in many places in the recent years – all wanting something different from me – but I do not understand what they are asking."

He continued, "I am not a horse like most others. This is what I have been trying to tell them. They may think I am dangerous and wish to hurt them, but this is not true. My message is misunderstood. I am a horse with an injury and this prevents me from doing the things they request. I have tried to communicate this many times. I throw my head in my trot before they ask me to canter to let them know that I am not capable without pain. Just the thought of the canter frightens me. I know in the eyes of the humans this makes me a lesser horse, but there are many other things I can do. I do not like the feeling of being an outcast – a problem horse that nobody wants or can figure out what to do with.

"Things are just so messed up. I cannot see a way out of this story that has been composed in a world I do not comprehend. There has been so much judgment placed upon me – but nobody has taken the time to get to know me. They want me to perform simple tasks that I am not capable of doing."

"So what now?" I asked. "What is it you need?"

"I need a fresh start. If I could find a way to tell them I want to be their horse. I want to be a part of their family. I have much to give if they can figure out a way to interpret my language. I cannot speak the words but if they take the time to look, I shall show them with my body. I will tell them all they need to know in order to see I am a horse of value and shall be like no other horse they have ever known. I may not carry them on my back literally but their weight they can place upon me in times of need. All I want is a place to call home, for people to see me for who I am and accept what it is that I have to offer. I am like no other horse; why can't they see this?"

"The human world is filled with the expectations of others and when they are not fulfilled they are discarded. This world moves very quickly and if we do not take the time to slow down and look closely, we may miss something unique. Sometimes our fears block our ability to communicate with you in a way you can understand. Unfortunately, this happens quite often. But, today – I hear you."

"Can you tell them this for me? Will you deliver my message? I shall be a horse they can depend upon. A horse they can be proud of. I will carry my family name proudly and deliver upon my promises – will you do this for me?"

"I will do my best – but the ultimate decision is not mine. I will tell them your story and of your desires, but I cannot make any promises. You are a beautiful being. Be true to who you are and teach the gifts that have been bestowed upon you."

"Gifts? I do not understand this. What they want I cannot give them."

"Sometimes a gift is not what they want – it is what they need. I shall deliver your message and I hope to see you again someday in the field you call home – with the family name you carry proudly."

As I exited the round pen I felt a surge of urgency – that I must deliver this message: He was simply misunderstood and his value had just not yet been discovered. This wondrously colored, full blood Appaloosa, with his wild eyes, was worth beginning anew. It was important to give what he needed and to take what he offered. This might take quite some time, but what things in their essence don't take time to reveal their truth and value?

I looked back one last time – not with sadness, but with gratitude – for we had found a way to see into both worlds where animals can be their true selves and live a life without barriers.

THE HORSE WITH LOTS OF POTENTIAL, By Ariana Strozzi Mazzucchi

One sunny morning in May I received a phone call from a woman named Mary. "I am calling to ask for your help. My daughter, Nicki, has a horse in Marin who is having problems. We have tried everything and we are looking for a horse whisperer and heard of you. Can you come out to the barn and see what can be done?"

The next day I drove to the hunter/jumper barn early. I arrived before mother and daughter to view the local surroundings of the barn. I noticed that the well-groomed horses were turned out in small paddocks (not much larger than their stalls) during the day. They all expressed a certain level of anxiety, from pacing the fence to tossing their heads in a desperate show of frustration. The stalls were the typical 12'x12' and the arenas were large but not fenced. Two round pens graced the grounds, but the fencing was below a horse's belly and thus was too low to let a horse move freely in the space. There was no place a person could let a stalled athlete go out for a run or buck to let out the pent-up energy that came with being stalled.

Nicki arrived and we went to Prince's paddock. After haltering him she took him out of the paddock, only to have him drag her from grass patch to grass patch.

"This is where the problem starts," I said. "First, you need to establish clear boundaries with him that you are his leader and dragging you about is not acceptable."

"No one has ever taught me how to lead a horse. I can jump a four-foot fence, but I don't know how to work with my horse on the ground."

I sighed a heavy sigh, as I have seen too often these days that young horsewomen and horsemen have not been taught how to properly handle their horses. They are taught to look pretty on their backs, to jump them over tall fences, but not how to establish a mutually respectful relationship built on trust and time.

I showed her how she needed to be the one who set the direction and purpose of walking together. After a few tries she established herself as the one who decided where the two would travel and when. We then went to the cross ties to groom and tack Prince. Once tied, he began to pin his ears, wring his tail, and toss his head. As Nicki began to groom him, he raised his hind leg in a threat to kick. His threats were exaggerated and painful to witness. His level of stress was significant, as if he were screaming to communicate, "Does anyone see I am having a problem here?" I watched and observed that he was not actually trying to hurt her, but was desperately trying to communicate to her his emotional pain.

"Yes, I can see he has a problem," I said as I came to his face and opened my palm. He put his muzzle in the palm of my hand and began licking me. He licked my hand for ten minutes as mother and daughter stood in awe.

"Wow. Why is he doing that?" Nicki asked.

"I think he is just wanting to be heard," I whispered as I continued to listen.

"Your horse is an athlete. He is tall and proud. He lives in a stall big enough to turn around in and his turnout is not sufficient for him to stretch and release the pent-up energy that he experiences from being so confined. It is unfortunate that there is nowhere on this ranch for you to let him stretch and run, to be a horse. So, I will teach you how to lunge him to help him let out his pent-up energy. This is essential for an athlete like him."

I taught Nicki how to lunge him before riding. I taught her how to listen to his energy level and not to get on him until his energy was quiet and connected. This light intervention did the trick for several months until I received another call from the mom. This time he had threatened to kick Nicki in his stall and had slammed his head over her head when she was trying to blanket him while he was eating his grain. It seemed obvious to me that for a horse like this, his stall was his only privacy. To be blanketed and handled in his stall, let alone when he was having his one and only treat of the day was understandably frustrating.

Nicki's mother again brought up that their trainer really believed that Nicki and this horse had *lots of potential* and he was frustrated that they were not doing better. At the same time he did not offer them any *off the jump field* advice. The words *lots of potential* rang in my head like a naggy mule. Nicki had often spoken how she was afraid of some of the taller jumps, but she was more afraid to tell her trainer about her fear. It stood to reason that Prince would refuse a jump when Nicki was afraid. If she was not sure about going over the jump, how could he be sure?

I tried to express to Nicki that it was important for her to notice when she felt afraid and to be able to admit it, for her own safety and for Prince's. Remember, I had not been hired as a coach or EGE professional; I had been hired as a horse whisperer to solve a problem right under the horse trainer's nose. Not an easy task. I offered a few more practices for talking with Prince and listening to his energy. I encouraged her to tell the trainer when she did not feel ready to go to the next challenge in her jumping lessons. I mentioned that taking any opportunity to get Prince in a larger field or pasture would be an enormous change for the better.

A few months passed until I received my third and last call from Nicki's mom: "Nicki has fallen off of Prince again and got a head concussion this time, we would like you to come out and discuss whether to sell Prince or keep trying to develop his potential."

There were those words again. I tried to fight back my frustration that these people only saw this horse as a potential ribbon winner. Prince lived a life that reminded me of a caged bird, or a beautiful slave. He had no sense of freedom. His owners ignored his outrage. He was listening to Nicki's fear.

The day she fell off, he had refused the jump three times. The trainer kept yelling, "Make him go over that jump." Nicki was afraid of the jump but continued to follow her trainer's orders, denying her fear, until finally Prince jumped over the fence. But because the horse and rider were not aligned, he tripped, which caused both him and her to fall.

Once I reached the stable, Nicki and I spent several hours talking about what had happened. I listened while wearing both my horsemanship hat and my EGE hat. She told me how things had been going along okay, and that most of the time she had been able to tell the trainer when she did not feel ready to go to the next jump height.

She was still feeling pressure from her mother and the trainer to compete. Their advice was to sell Prince and get another horse with *more potential*. She was conflicted because she knew that Prince's problem was her problem and she did not want to abandon him. But she did not want to stop showing, either. Or perhaps she did not want to disappoint her mother and the trainer.

When I spoke to her mother, I spoke firmly. "I hope you can see that your trainer does not care about your daughter's safety. What he cares about is Prince's potential and his own success as a horse trainer. If you care more about showing and what your trainer wants, then perhaps it is best to sell Prince. If, on the other hand, you care about how your daughter develops her relationship with her horse and the relationship between horse and girl is a priority, then keep Prince and experiment with some other disciplines besides jumping."

I was disappointed to hear that they decided to sell Prince, but happy to hear that he was flourishing with his new owner.

Several years later, I received a call from Nicki, now grown and graduated from college. She wanted to learn more about EGE as a possible career. She had not ridden in years but still felt a deep connection to horses that she wanted to rekindle. At this time, we were able to discuss the deeper ramifications of her relationship with Prince.

While I was hired as a horse whisperer, my EGE wisdom kept telling me that something else in Nicki's personal life was being reflected in her relationship with her horse. I was not granted permission to step into that conversation at the time, so I stayed in my role as horse professional. I had always suspected that part of the relationship dynamic with her and Prince had to do with her underlying feelings around her mother and her trainer. I wondered if some of Prince's aggression towards her came from her lack of being able to be authentic with these two elder role models.

Hopefully, this story illustrates the invisible separation between being in horsemanship mind and being in EGE mind. I will discuss in later chapters some tools for navigating between a horsemanship model and an EGE model.

SUMMARY

- EGE is about self-development, not training horses.

- What is happening on the inside (spirit) of a person directly impacts the horse and is its primary source of information.

- EGE does not focus on the tools and techniques of horsemanship but rather on how the horse is mirroring the energetic dynamics of how a person is relating to his or her own story and how the person navigates his or her relationships.

- EGE requires that the horsewoman shift her perspective from the horse as a tool for her to control, to the horse as a sensate being who mirrors her own deeper intentions.

- Horses can teach us how to change our perspective on social interaction, leadership, and coordination. We yearn to break away from dominant-subordinate relationships and to learn to create mutually reciprocal relationships in our families, our love relationships, and our work relationships.

THE FIVE ELEMENTS OF EGE

The Horse As Guide

*The Facilitator Creates
an Experiential Learning Environment*

The Change Process

A Somatic, Non-linear Approach to Learning

*The Magical and Mysterious Wisdom
of the Natural World*

The Horse As Guide

HORSES LIVE IN THE MOMENT

Horses are often described as magical, mysterious, practical, impractical, scary, safe, beautiful, dangerous, funny, loving, kind, and even smelly. Horses make great teachers and healers for so many reasons it is hard to know where to start. We begin with the premise that the horse can connect us to the non-verbal world of our imagination, our sixth sense, and our intuitive abilities.

The horse is a somatic being that embodies its physical, emotional, and mental states transparently at each moment. The horse does not hide its feelings. The horse is completely authentic. There is no such thing as an inauthentic horse. The horse does not doubt how it feels. It might doubt humans, but it does not doubt its own experience.

The horse is emotion in full glory, one moment tranquil and the next scared, defiant, pissy, loving. The horse is not only *in the moment* the horse *is* the moment. The horse mirrors present time, present states of emotion, present energetic tones and attitudes. The horse even mirrors energetic memories of past experiences, but always as they are being remembered in the present moment. Sometimes these memories are created through memories held in the mind and sometimes in the memories that are held in the body.

The horse is whimsical, fiery, brave, free, enslaved. The horse embraces our experience, mirroring our space of possibility or our dungenous darkness. The horse meets us at the frontier of our own making. The horse becomes us and we become the horse.

The horse teaches us how to live in the present moment of our experience. Horses help us take notice when we fall into old stories of the past and are forgetting to dream our future. By teaching us to be in the moment, the horse reminds us to listen to and respect our experience. To listen to what our intuition and non-linear perspective is saying.

59

HORSES ARE NON-JUDGMENTAL

Two significant factors are unique to the EGE process and are the direct result of the horses' non-judgmental nature. One is that people will accept feedback from a horse that they will not accept from other humans. Two is that people want to change for the horse's sake much more than they want to change for themselves.

People from all demographics and walks of life know that the horse has no agenda with them. The horse does not judge them. Humans seem to inherently accept that the horse is mirroring them and at the same time do not feel shamed by the horse. During EGE (that is well facilitated), we can bypass the human clutter of fear of judgment, separation, and exclusion. I have never heard a person say in an EGE process, "The horse just doesn't understand me, or doesn't see me."

In the EGE process the horse offers an unbiased response to humans. Complexity arises as to whether or not the human facilitator and client can also remain somewhat unbiased in the presence of horses. Perhaps this is one of the significant teaching points horses can demonstrate. What does it mean to be unbiased?

One aspect of a horse's unbiased approach to humans is its lack of judgment. Horses do not fix a person in a specific box or stereotype. They do not place labels on people based on past performance or experience. They do not see an autistic child as deformed, or a sad person as unworthy. They do not categorize people with negative or positive assessments. They simply follow their own curiosity and sense of engagement that directly relates to the person in a specific moment in time.

Humans are the judgmental animals. We rate each other. We categorize, label, and fixate people with our assessments. We think our assessments are truths. We think we know and have the right to assess others. We base our assessments on what we've been told, or what we think is *right* or *wrong* – a pivotal aspect of judgment. We live in a false reality of right versus wrong. For some people, these judgments are so necessary to their concept of reality that they live in a black-and-white world with little room to imagine new possibilities.

Extreme words such as *always* and *never* are common judgmental words.

Horses do not live in *right* and *wrong*. They do not live in *always* and *never*. They live in the moment of their experience. At the same time, they are unsentimental, which contributes to their ability to offer frank and unbiased feedback.

Horses have an amazing willingness to accept. Horses offer a sense of compassion that most humans wish they could find within themselves. Compassion requires a lack of judgment or moral assessment, which makes it one of the more difficult of human traits to master. Compassion allows the possibility that we can change our assessments and the assessments of others.

HORSES LISTEN TO ENERGY

Another key component of the EGE process that is important to understand is that the horse's primary form of communication occurs in the non-linguistic, non-linear realm of energy. Horses listen to the energetic qualities of one's body language, mood, internal stories, attitude, and general state of being. Horses see energy in its raw, unedited form. Horses can sense images or pictorial representations of a person's inner state of mind.

Horses are giant energy communicators. Like most wild animals, they rely on their instincts and energetic responses to changes in the energy of their environment in order to determine if they are safe or need to flee or fight. They trust their feelings. They make decisions based on how they feel, not what they think. They do not doubt their feelings like we do.

When horses sense an increase in energy in their environment, they respond to it. They allow (when they're free) the energy to move through them. They mirror the tone and quality of that energy. If a person in their presence becomes afraid and tense in the body, the horse mirrors the fear by becoming tense as well. Every movement that the horse makes is a response to the energy in its environment, which includes the participant(s), facilitator, other horses, and greater surroundings.

For example, if I were in a horsemanship mindset, when a horse swishes its tail, I would say, "That horse is swishing its tail at a fly." When we are in an EGE process, a tail swishing may be in response to the tone or quality of a person's underlying mood or attitude. A ringing tail swish may mirror the irritation that a person is experiencing internally as he or she reflects on a particular event or situation. A swishy tail could be a reflection of an energetic unease, irritation, or even anger.

When we're in passive relationship with horses where the horse can come and go as it pleases, we study the energy of our relationship to the horses and the horse's relationship to us. We experience and explore the energetic tone and quality of the horse's and the human's inner experience. If there is a lot of extra energy, the horse might run around the arena. She might buck. She might fart. She might toss her head. She might stomp her feet. She might yawn or paw the ground.

The EGE facilitator and client notice the horse's actions and explore how it relates to the client's session.

We tend to overuse the rational mind, giving it almost complete control to interpret our experience. As mentioned earlier, during EGE it is fundamental to switch the emphasis from the logical process to the more intuitive or sensate wisdom that lives in the animal body.

Horses don't place a value judgment on the quality or tone of energy. They don't mentally interpret, they respond. They don't see the energy as good or bad energy; they don't even necessarily see it as positive or negative. We don't have good words or distinctions to describe what is actually occurring here, yet it is one of the most natural and basic processes happening around us all of the time.

The more one studies EGE, the more one realizes that our verbal language pales in comparison to the richness of the senses. Because we are judgmental animals, we tend to quantify and qualify energy into specific definitions such as anxiety, anger, boredom, and fear. By labeling and quantifying how our body is responding energetically to stimuli, we are forming conclusions and judgments about ourselves and others before we even have the chance to really experience the emotion before the judgment. We tend to miss many alternative, even healthier perspectives in the rush to make a conclusion. Even then, the words we use to describe our experience tend to have negative or positive connotations.

We can learn from horses how to listen to the energy and the quality or tone of the energy that underlies our current emotions. Before we label our experience with words such as anger or anxiety, we can acknowledge that our body is going through an energetic change. Our heart rate increases and we feel the increased energy flow through the body. Instead of rushing to our human labels to define these sensations, we can become more like a horse and just be present to the increase in energy. Once we place a label on the energy we are experiencing, a whole new set of interpretations and stories develops. Some of these are not effective and may be misinterpretations of the experience of the energetic change that is present.

When people label themselves as bored or depressed, the horse may simply be living in the presence of a lack of energy or a dulling of the senses. Depression can often be an unconscious dulling of the senses to ward off deeper feelings and spiritual angst. When we are doing EGE, horses offer us the possibility of suspending our quick assessments that what we are experiencing is bad and encourage us to just be present to the quality of energy we are experiencing and see if we can find more information about the quality of our experience before we categorize and quantify it. In this way, we can ultimately create many more healthy interpretations than rushing to the most negative, judgmental one.

Sometimes during an EGE session, a person may be smiling or joking around, making light of his or her experience. If the person is expressing a light attitude on the outside, while inside feeling inadequate or angry, the horse reads this as being inauthentic or not genuine. The horse is listening to the deeper feelings of inadequacy. When horses experience a person as being inauthentic, or not *telling the truth*, they feel unsafe and may become aggressive toward the person, as if to say, "You are not telling the truth; therefore I can't trust you and it is unsafe for me to have you around right now because you are not in touch with your experience. And if you are not in touch with your experience and danger comes over the hill, you may not respond well and may put me in danger too. Therefore, you need to get out of my space."

Sometimes a person does not have a clear sense of her own frustration. There may be too much rational chatter interrupting her ability to listen to her spiritual longing. In this case, a horse will often walk away or disengage with the person, as if to say, "You are really in your head right now and your rationalizations are not interesting or pertinent to what your deeper conversation wants to be."

The magical part of EGE comes to the foreground when, by just being in the presence of a horse without too much talking or dialogue, humans can get in touch with the authentic conversation and find the courage to face their dilemmas.

When working with teams, horses quickly suss out when members of a team are not energetically aligned with each other or with the purpose of their interactions. Horses reveal through their energetic responses the quality of energy associated with the lack of alignment. If one person on a team is in a mood of resentment, horses will mirror that resentment. Sometimes they will even physically remove the resentful person from the rest of the group, as if to say, "You are not being part of the group right now." If a person in the group were to say that to the resentful person, that person might become more resentful and reply, "Yes, I am" or "It's your fault." When a horse says it, the person is more likely to accept that he or she is indeed not feeling like part of the group and be less likely to get defensive and blaming.

Horses offer amazing new insights into how much of our human interactions are actually occurring on a non-verbal level. They help us learn to listen not just to words said, but also to the mood or tone of the conversation and the person with whom we are engaging. This topic will be discussed further in later chapters.

The horse's keen ability to reveal the energetic tone of the individuals and the group is a great asset for the EGE professional. In order to determine energetic tone, great skill is required. This skill comes from experience and trusting that the horses are indeed mirroring the essence of the conversation that is occurring without words.

I remember the day this important concept really hit home for me. I was in Minnesota several years ago doing a three-day Leadership & Horses™ program. It was the first day and we had completed introductions. The group of participants was lined up along a small arena and I was going to move the horses around to illustrate herd dynamics. I had about five horses in the arena and had never worked with them before. They lived in the same pasture on the ranch and were used to being together. All of the sudden they started getting really agitated and going faster and faster. The gelding started getting really aggressive with one of the older mares, biting her butt and rushing at her until she almost fell down.

I could feel the participants getting worried and holding their breath. I can usually go into the center of the arena, take a couple deep breaths, and the horses will relax. I tried and was surprised that the horses were not responsive. They were not connected because they were in a very hyper-alert state. Feeling the tension build inside and outside of the arena, I asked the participants to take three deep breaths collectively. We all took three deep breaths and relaxed our shoulders and the horses stopped. Everyone was amazed. As the EGE professional, I wondered if indeed there was a person there who had such a contraction of energy that it was scaring the horses. I was looking for a correlation between the horses' behavior and the energy of the group and/or an individual in the group.

One woman was very tense and her body was quite contracted. It turned out that she was an extremely self-critical individual and whenever she would get overly self-judgmental, the horses would get more aggressive with each other. Because I listened to the dynamics of the herd on the first day, I was able to have a heightened awareness and listening for her situation.

HORSES AND HUMANS ARE SO SIMILAR

Humans and horses share the same social instincts, which function to increase both individual and group survival. Horses are born with an innate desire to be part of the herd. A lone horse does not last long on the prairie, becoming an easy target for predators. It needs the protection of the whole herd to increase its chances of survival. In turn, the herd depends on each individual horse to contribute to the survival of the whole. It is imperative for each horse to find its place in the herd. This desire translates into an animal that wants to be of service, accounting for the ease in which horses have participated in our lives for thousands of years. It is only through confusion and abuse that a horse loses this natural desire to cooperate and serve.

Humans are also born with an innate desire to be part of the tribe (herd). To be part of the herd means that a person is a valued member and the herd needs that person's unique contribution to increase its overall survivability. The sense of *being needed* encourages a healthy self-image and an increased desire to be of service. Every one of us privately longs to be valuable, to be of service, and to have an identity in our greater community. This makes sense, since the more social value we have, the more likely we will be helped by others in a time of crisis. The instinct to contribute is so deeply rooted that it is difficult to locate in our cognitive thought process, but if we listen deeply, we can feel this drive deep in our body and in our subconscious mind.

As social animals, we need to *fit in*. There is nothing more satisfying than contributing to others and feeling *needed*. Just like the workhorse, we wonder, *Am I doing a good job?* When our leaders and elders tell us we are needed and what we have to offer is important and unique, we thrive. When we aren't getting feedback that we're doing good work, we lose confidence in ourselves. The resentful horse or resigned employee is the embodiment of an individual who has lost a sense of value. She is not sure she is needed any more. She does her work, but deep inside she doesn't feel that she is part of the herd.

In the EGE process, horses can help us find a better understanding of our social nature and its significance in our interactions with other humans. The need to be needed and to make a contribution is essential to a person feeling balance and fulfillment in life and becomes a pivotal aspect of the EGE process. In addition, the horse's similar need for social interaction allows for the fertile ground of EGE to exist. It is in the very process of the social engagement between horse and human that the reflections, insights, and conversations about life and living arise.

To better understand the horse's point of view, let's imagine that if a horse could talk in human words, he might say the following:

I am a social animal. This means that I am born with an innate desire to be part of something (the herd). I need to be with other horses in order to feel safe. It scares me to be alone, physically, mentally, and spiritually.

- Are you another horse?

- What are we going to do together?

- What is your place in the herd?

- What is your place in relation to me?

I am a hierarchal animal. Hierarchy is established in order for the herd to coordinate physically and without thought in response to perturbations and danger. The lead mare as the direction setter is responsible for deciding what direction to go in, and how fast. The second and third mares push on the lead mare with feedback about food and water resources and environmental changes. The other mares in the herd often will notice dangerous stimuli or changes in the environment first, but the lead mare decides what to do about it. In situations of danger, the stallion bunches the other horses together in dense masses to collectively avoid predation.

- I need to know your physical boundaries so that if danger is present, I know my place in relation to you.

- Do you know what to do?

- Are you the lead mare? Are you the lead stallion?

- Do you know what you care about?

- Do you know your role in the herd?

- Can I trust you to be consistent, reliable, and sincere?

- Are you confident about what you are asking of me?

- Do you believe what you are asking from me is possible?

- I need to be part of things.

- I resent being a tool.

HORSES TEACH SOMATIC, SENSATE AWARENESS

The horse is a fully embodied, somatic being. He depends on his intuition and feelings for survival. He does not apply thoughtfulness before he acts. He acts first; maybe he thinks later. If a horse could talk, he might say something like:

- I listen with my senses, not my intellect.

- What is the quality or tone of the energy?

- Is there too much energy, or not enough?

- What direction is the energy going in?

- How do you feel right now?

- Can you feel me?

- Are you trustworthy?

- Are you being authentic?

- What do you care about?

- You need to be responsible for your own energy.

- What's all that busy-ness in your head, it is distracting.

- If you want me to participate one hundred percent, then I need you to be one hundred percent present as well.

HORSES LOOK FOR CLEAR ROLES IN RELATIONSHIP

Wild horse herds are comprised of bands. Bands are comprised of seven to eight horses with a lead mare, a lead stallion, and several other mares (each with her own role and responsibilities) and their foals. In everyday conversation we usually use the term herd, when in fact we mean band. So for the purposes of this book, I will continue to refer to the band as a herd.

Even in domesticity, horses tend to form herds with intricate relationships between each horse. Due to horses' social and hierarchal instincts, it is important for the group as a whole to know each horse's role in the herd. Each horse has a certain set of responsibilities within its role that are designed to promote the survivability of the whole. Each horse's role and associated responsibilities are regularly re-negotiated as the energy of their surrounding environment changes.

For example, when horses begin to feel that a person in the human group is not fitting in, whether because of self-imposed separation or because of non-verbal competition between individuals within the group, the horses will begin re-negotiating their roles in relation to each other. In its instinctive form, this assures that the role of each horse within the herd is clear in case the herd as a whole needs to coordinate for safety of the whole.

It is as if the horses are saying, "Hey, something is changing in the environment and we may no longer be safe. Are our roles and relationships clear, so if we need to flee we know our place in relation together? For if we have to flee, there will be no time to argue about whose responsible for what role."

Another important aspect of the horse's instinct for roles and relationship is that horses are hard wired with a need to know who the leader of the herd is. This sets up a rich metaphor for the concept of leadership as a form of relationship. When an EGE facilitator has an individual engage with a horse in an active exercise like leading in hand, the horse needs to know who is leading. It is as if the horse is saying, "Are you leading? Do you know who you are and what you care about?" and if the horse is unsure or the individual is not clearly being a leader – the direction setter – then the horse will become the leader. A dialogue and set of practices can then ensue in which the individual practices embodying a leadership presence that is centered on goals and ambitions.

Let's take a look at some of the common roles horse have within a herd, followed by some examples of how herd dynamics can offer valuable lessons in human dynamics.

ROLES OF HORSES THAT RELATE TO HUMANS

The Lead Mare

In horsemanship models, we often hear, "You have to be the leader of the horse." What does that mean exactly? Why do all horsemanship models require that the horse person establish himself/herself as the leader? The answer to this question relates to both the horse's and the human's social instinct. In a social system, there needs to be one ultimate decision maker. In many modern leadership theories, we like to explore concepts of shared leadership, but one thing stays true to form. When it comes time to make a decision for a specific action, one individual declares the direction of the group's coordinated actions.

In the United States we designate the president to play this role. In the United Kingdom the prime minister is the direction setter and in a horse herd, the lead mare takes this role.

I like to think of the leader's role more as that of the direction setter. In human leadership, we tend to see leadership as a top-down system. Our notion of leadership tends to view the leader as the dominant one. When studying leadership theory, humans tend to think of being a leader as being the "boss." Even in the most educated groups of humans, we tend to think that a leader needs to be smarter than, more than, better than the rest. This immediately implies that everyone else is less than.

This concept of the leader's role and everyone else's role in relation to the leader is narrow and contracted. Studying leadership through equine herd dynamics allows humans to begin to see leadership in a new light. We throw out the human concept of dominant/subordinate roles, and begin to view the leader's role as just one of the many roles within a group of social animals. In its truest sense, the leader of the herd's main role is to set the direction, pace, and course of action for the group.

In a horse herd, the lead mare is the direction setter. When danger approaches and the herd gets scared, they all look at her and ask, "What do we do?" She says, "We're going to go down that hill, this fast and this far." She may not be the one in the front, but the other horses follow her movements, direction, and pace. Her job is not necessarily to scout out danger; her job is to make a decision about what to do about the situation at hand. Is the perturbation that the herd is experiencing dangerous or serious enough to take action?

Observing the lead mare and her role within the herd provides rich conversations about leadership and the role of the leader. At an individual level, the lead mare embodies the same attributes an individual needs to embody to effectively lead his or her life in the direction the person declares he or she wants to go.

In my work with leaders, the EGE process reveals many valuable metaphors, including:

- The lead mare (as leader) is not the busiest one. In fact, the lead mare is one of the most energy efficient of all the horses. She does not busy herself with minor details and fluctuations within the herd politics.

- The lead mare is not always out in front. Metaphor: To be a leader does not mean being ahead of everyone else. Sometimes being a leader means following the nuances of the whole.

- The lead mare is not responsible for keeping everyone else in line. That is the role the lead male plays. The lead mare and lead stallion play complimentary, not competitive roles. This implication is very valuable in exploring relationship dynamics.

The Lead Male

The lead male's role in a herd is to protect the herd from danger. When the horses are feeling a need to move away quickly, he supports the lead mare by pushing the other horses in the herd to get together and follow the same path. You will often see him pushing the mares from behind. He's biting them and pushing them to become a dense ball of flesh. The instinct to come together in times of danger is very similar to the human's instinct. Deer are different. Deer scatter. There's something important in this distinction.

The lead male acts more like the manager, making sure the group is sticking together and listening to the direction the lead mare sets.

The Sentinel

The horse that seems to not fit in, I call her the sentinel or barometer. A horse that looks like she doesn't fit in the herd, the one who is not politicking with other horses, tends to be playing a very important role for the group as a whole. Rather than seeing her as "the loner," we can appreciate her as the one who is listening and attending to the energetics of the peripheral environment. She may be the first to see the predator around the corner because she is already on the periphery of the herd.

In the wild when resources start to dry up, the sentinel will start to become more assertive and will begin to push into the herd, which sends a cue to the lead mare that she needs to pay attention.

In the EGE process the sentinel provides a re-interpretation of roles. A person who assesses the sentinel as being *left out* or *not part of the herd* learns that indeed she is an important member of the herd even though she is not lead mare. Often a person making this assessment is revealing something about his or her inner self-identification. Usually people who are focused or interested in the sentinel identify with her. If they interpret her as being *left out*, they are implying how they themselves may be feeling in relation to the social group.

The EGE facilitator can help these people re-interpret their roles as being just as important as the lead mare's role. If we can begin to see that each horse plays a contributory role to the whole, individuals can find more self-respect and more respect for others in their social circles. Think about it: A herd does not need lots of leaders. A herd needs different individuals attending to different aspects of the group experience.

The Nurturer

Some of the mares in the herd are less interested in the hustle and bustle of the herd politics and more focused on raising the young and teaching proper social manners. These mares are vital to the nuances of the herd's stability. While the other mares are moved by the lead mare, they have a grounded presence and a confidence that provides a mirror for a person with a similar nature. In the EGE process, people can find a sense of acceptance for *who they are* rather than trying to be someone they are not. This insight can also be useful in teams where everyone is trying to be just like the lead mare and subsequently wondering why they are not effective as a whole.

In a human group, the nurturer may appear to be the group cheerleader, attending to the mood of the group. Her unique individual character places an emphasis on how the individuals within the group are getting along. She is not as focused on maintaining the vision of the group, but rather sees that the success of the group depends on the relationships between the individuals. This is a very important and different role than that of the lead stallion.

The nurturer in a human group may also express a special interest in developing the younger, more inexperienced members of the group and making sure they have support and encouragement.

Lead Mares in Training

In the horse herd, the authority of the leader is never taken for granted. It is not a static state achieved once and always held, but is regularly defended by the leader and recurrently reassessed by the herd members. The mares in secondary and tertiary leadership roles – lead mares in training – tend to be the busiest members of the herd. They spend more time than the other horses at politicking for roles and position. They often push on the other horses in the herd to see if they can establish more authority. They want respect from the other horses, but don't quite embody the confidence and follow-through of the lead mare.

The busy-ness of these mares is actually an important component of the overall survivability of the herd. It is their antics that urge the lead mare to stay at her best. It is when a lead mare is no longer physically able to hold her role that one of these mares in training will become the new lead mare.

I find this metaphor very powerful when I am working with teams. Often in teams, the future up-and-coming leaders are seen as nuisances. They are always pushing and striving for identity and respect, but may not yet embody the skills they need to achieve these things. So rather than being seen as future assets to the team, they are seen as irritating. When the team leader is able to shift his interpretation from seeing these individuals as frustrating to work with to accepting them as future leaders, a whole new set of agreements can occur.

In this new interpretation, the team is able to give these future leaders more responsibility so they can practice taking the responsibility they are asking to take. Once these future leaders are given some responsibilities, especially ones that have some level of risk associated with them, they become loyal, hard-working members of the team.

HERD DYNAMICS AND EGE

The quest for position in our social communities is similar to the questing among horses for herd position. Observing horse herds and the roles of each individual gives us valuable clues to our own social, hierarchal nature. In the EGE process, the facilitator can encourage participants to observe and explore the roles of horses within the herd to gain insights into their own patterns of relating to others. In order for a facilitator to encourage exploration of roles and responsibilities in the human group, the facilitator must have a good working knowledge of herd dynamics and an understanding of how these dynamics also occur in human herds.

It is interesting to note that in the human sciences, it has been determined that a manager within a company can only manage up to eight people. And the definition of the word, "manage," in its original translation, meant, "to train or direct a horse." Thus there are numerous opportunities to explore human dynamics of relating and forming teams through the observation and exploration of herd dynamics. Since our social and hierarchical instincts are so similar to those of horses, the metaphors tend to be quite apparent and informative.

Individuals or teams can gain valuable new insights into how roles and relationships are being formed before any words are actually spoken. Depending on the EGE facilitator's goals – what concepts the facilitator wants to explore – observing herd dynamics can take several different tacks. One tack could be individual style or a person's natural desire to be in a certain role within social groups. Some people are natural leaders, while others prefer to take a more peripheral role. Another tack could be team dynamics, how teams are built, how individuals negotiate, what different roles need to be in place for an effective team, how competing roles cause breakdowns in team cohesion, etc.

For example, in a team with a history of infighting for authority, participants can realize that it is more valuable to create complimentary roles within their teams rather than roles that overlap or cause competition. Through dialogue and discussion, the facilitator can help to reveal the misconceptions a team may have about roles and responsibilities.

Another topic of exploration when observing herd dynamics is noticing how horses negotiate with each other and then reflecting on how we as humans negotiate. For example, when observing horses negotiating with each other, the facilitator can expose how often horses need to re-negotiate their roles. Even slight changes in the environment can cause an urge in the herd to make sure their roles and relations are in order. Also, how they negotiate is of particular interest. In human groups, when we need to re-establish roles, we tend to hold on to past conversations and interactions, which often results in holding grudges or bracing for another breakdown in communication.

Observing how horses negotiate, we note that the horses may reinforce their position, but then let it go. They do not hold grudges. They do not brace, expecting the other horse to confront them again. They let things go, and start anew. What if humans could do that?

Through observation and discussion of herd dynamics, participants will often identify more with one role than another. The facilitator can use the power of projection to learn about each individual's self-perceptions. For example, during an observation of a group of horses, one client may identify with the lead mare, while another participant may identify with the sentinel. The EGE facilitator can respond by encouraging the power of embracing our uniqueness and encouraging self-acceptance as a way of strengthening the whole. A key learning point in this facilitation is that we are not the same, nor should we try to be someone we are not.

The way a herd reacts to a group of people will tell the EGE professional a lot about the interpersonal dynamics of the individuals in the group and the group as a collective whole. When there is discord or lack of alignment in the group (it could be just one person not feeling included), the horses will tend to increase their negotiations and herd dynamics. When everyone in the group is engaged and open to learning, the horses will often be calm and relaxed.

It is important to note that there are a lot of other factors involved. This is where the skill level of the EGE professional becomes a significant factor. It is up to the EGE professional to be filtering out larger influences in the environment, including time of day, the horses' usual routine, and the weather in addition to group dynamics and individual variation.

HORSES ARE NATURALLY CURIOUS

One of my most favorite aspects of horses is their curiosity and playfulness. No matter how badly they are treated or how hard their history may have been, they just keep coming back with a sense of freedom for adventure and discovery. This kind of curious fascination with the world around us allows us to open our perspective and create new stories for our lives.

To access the spirit requires imagination and curiosity, a form of *not knowing and not requiring an answer*. As Henry Poincare, a colleague of Einstein, wrote, "It is by logic that we prove, but by intuition that we discover." The native imagination begins in the realm of feeling and sensory awareness and emerges into consciousness through an ability to suspend certainty. It is in this precise way that horses can become our teachers, offering us a whole new world of sensory awareness where new insight and new interpretations can form.

HORSE TIME

Horse time is a valuable metaphor to remember when practicing horsemanship in general and especially in EGE. Horse time is generally a slower pace in that we allow the horse up to four times as long to respond to our cues than we usually do. We are so used to asking and expecting an immediate response. Rushing or being out of horse time does not allow either the horse or the human, whoever is the one responding, to adequately integrate incoming messages and formulate a response. Learning to communicate in horse time is an immensely valuable tool in building trust and effective coordination for both horses and humans.

Remember, following horse time doesn't n l ecessarily mean moving at a quarter of your usual pace or sense of time; it has more to do with slowing down to develop your appreciation of your senses.

Specifically it means slowing down your mind's interpretation of what is happening and what assessments you are forming. It means listening to the body – yours, others', and the horse's. It means letting your other senses of sight, smell, touch, intuition, kinesthesia, and anything non-linear come alive and have time to actually sense.

HEART ENERGY

Energy emanates from our heart in a rhythmic pattern, generating the largest electromagnetic field in the body. The electric field generated by the heart is about sixty times greater in amplitude than the electric field of the brain. Research has shown that when people are in proximity of one another, a transfer of electromagnetic energy occurs. In other words, we are affecting and being affected by others in our presence.

We are familiar with the importance of our heart in terms of our physical health. We take our heart rate during physical exercise or when we go to the doctor. The Institute for Heart Math has been studying heart energy and how the electromagnetic field of the heart relates to emotions for many years. Their research shows that the heart has its own intelligence, complete with its own neurotransmitters and hormones. They have shown that positive, loving emotions such as care, compassion, non-judgment, and appreciation have a measurable effect on our blood chemistry. Feeling any of these positive emotions results in increased levels of anti-aging and disease-fighting antibodies. On the other hand, negative emotions such as anger, blaming, and criticism lead to more stress and a reduced immune response.

They even go so far as to say that an individual's thoughts, attitudes, and emotions also emit energetic fields. The term "heart intelligence" refers to the flow of awareness, understanding, and intuition we experience when the mind and emotions are in coherent alignment with the heart. Think about the saying, "Follow your heart." Why do we say that? What does it mean?

Heart energy or the heart field is a very important component of EGE work that can be explored further. Without even knowing this research existed, I have witnessed since the late 1980s a consistent energetic field of communication that occurs between horses and humans. When I get asked the question, "Wow, how does this EGE stuff really work?" I think the electromagnetic field of the horse's heart intelligence plays a significant role. When my clients are around horses (as opposed to being in an office), they tend to emote more often and sooner. They tend to say things like, "Wow, I didn't expect to become overwhelmed with emotion." I often respond, "Actually, in the presence of horses it is pretty normal."

Even in the classroom, when we begin a new class and people are introducing themselves, this energetic coherence-balancing act is already beginning. The horses do not even need to be near the people. People just need to be in the general proximity of horses to begin to feel a shift in their authentic expression, or their *heart's longing*.

Without performing extensive research, we do know that the average horse's heart weighs approximately nine or ten pounds, which is nine to ten times the size of the human heart. The human heart's electrical field is sixty times greater than the electrical field generated by the brain. The human heart's magnetic field is five thousand times stronger than the brain's magnetic field and can be detected several feet beyond the body in all directions. Multiply this by ten, and you begin to get a sense of the underlying *mystery and magic* of EGE.

CORRECTING THE PREDATOR/PREY MYTH

Many of today's modern horse professionals are saying that the dynamic tension between our differences, the horse as a prey animal and the human as a predator, explains why our relationships with horses work. They explain that it is the horses' prey nature that causes the horses to fear us. Yet, having worked with many predator and prey species in my zoology career, I would have to say that any wild animal fears us in a similar way. If you were to put a coyote or mountain lion in a round pen or a confine it to a stall, it would resort to behaviors very similar to those we commonly see in the horse.

In addition, these equine professionals are misinformed and misusing a specific term common in the science of biology. The zoological definition of *prey* is an animal that is killed and eaten by another species. The definition of *predator* is an animal that preys upon, destroys, or devours another. The predator is a carnivorous animal whose entire muscular skeletal system is designed to hunt and kill its prey. The prey animal can be either a herbivorous or carnivorous species that is found commonly in the local environment of the predator species.

Predation is a way of life in which food is chiefly obtained by killing animals. The relationship between a predator and its prey contributes to ecosystem equilibrium. In wild populations, predation plays an important role in maintaining the population size of prey animals and since predators tend to only take the weak, old, or sick, it helps to assure strong, healthy populations of prey species. The coyote and the rabbit are a good example in that the coyote's role as predator is fundamentally important to managing the population of rabbits.

The predator-prey relationship is complex and important, but it does not explain our relationship to the horse. As human beings, we may become *predatorial* when we attempt to manage the control of a species by killing and eating it. We would have to have an intertwined history of killing horses and eating them in order for a horse to consider us its predator. In the field of biology, we are not considered a predator. We are omnivorous animals. While we hunt and are also preyed upon, we do not rely on a specific predator-prey relationship in order to exist.

The wild horse, and particularly the domestic horse, does not see us as a lion threatening its survival by trying to eat it for dinner. Instead, the horse senses our intention to separate it from its herd, to capture it and domesticate it. Yes, the horse is afraid, but his prey nature does not explain his fear. Perhaps he wants to flee simply because his instinctive fear is that he will be isolated (a terrifying notion to a horse because of its social nature), and that we will aggress upon him and dominate him, forcing him to acquiesce and relinquish his free spirit and natural ways.

Even a herd of horses can feel when the human is consumed by his/her desire to control and manipulate others. The horse sees this as being completely out of integrity with the natural *way of things*. The more the human imposes his or her will upon the horse, the more the human dominates the situation, the more out of integrity with *the whole* he or she becomes. And thus the horse is driven into a deep, instinctive fear for survival. In this state, the horse can be completely engulfed by his fear. His fear for survival can become so predominant that the horse can actually fall into a psycho-spiritual death, in which the horse either loses his will to live or his spirit becomes lost and he literally goes crazy loco, and consequently unmanageable.

Some wild horses have been killed by humans in an effort to manage their populations, but the ancient bond between man and horse far supersedes these atrocities. The horse in ancient times would often follow the human tribe from location to location, drawn together rather than apart. Domestic horses when born in captivity do not see the human as a predator, but as another herd member.

Let's remember that as humans we are omnivorous animals, historically combining several strategies of hunting and gathering to survive. The raccoon is also an omnivorous animal, and we do not consider the raccoon to be a predator. So why are we assuming that we are predators to the horse? The horse is strictly herbivorous, a natural prey animal for carnivorous predators, but so are gazelles, zebras, and deer. Why then have we been unsuccessful in domesticating these other prey animals? Why is our relationship with the horse so unique?

Our successful domestication of and subsequent relationship to horses cannot be explained by their prey nature. So rather than focus on a predator-prey relationship that does not exist between man and horse, perhaps it is better to ask, "How does the horse's sensate, somatic nature impact our relationship with them? How are we similar in the way we see the world?"

Perhaps the domestic horse isn't afraid that we are going to eat him, he is afraid that we will exile him, that we will not accept him into the herd, or that we are being intensely inauthentic and cannot be trusted. When we approach the horse as if to dominate it and impose our will upon it, it may resist such subordination, for inside it still knows it is free. Isn't that free will in a horse, their sense of freedom, part of what we fall in love with? What we may be interpreting as *prey* responses to our loud gestures and dominating tactics is really a startled response questioning our lack of connection. I have seen many a horse that is gentle with one person and completely terrified of another. I am sure if you have spent any significant time around horses that you have seen this too. And you know in your heart it is not because the horse is a prey animal and we are the predator.

If the EGE professional focuses on asking the question, "What do horses and humans have *in common* that allow us the potential to truly unite and blend our core energies together to create something larger than either individual alone could manifest?" we find that horses and humans have a pre-verbal understanding of each other driven by similar social, hierarchal strategies for survival.

Of the 4,250 mammalian species, we have only successfully domesticated fourteen of them, and only five are important on a global scale: the horse, the pig, the sheep, the cow, and the goat. Jared Diamond, in *Guns, Germs, and Steel*, writes in detail on this subject. His studies on the domestication of animals clarify the unique virtues that allow us to develop long-term bonds with horses.

One significant factor is their reasonable disposition. Out of the eight species of wild horses and their relatives, only two have been domesticated: the horse and the North African ass. Despite numerous attempts to domesticate the other six, they are too aggressive and antagonistic towards humans, whereas horses are curious and willing to give us a chance.

Diamond goes on to note that the majority of domesticated large mammals have three similar social characteristics: They live in herds, they maintain an ordered hierarchy among herd members, and different herds occupy overlapping home ranges, rather than exclusive territories.

SUMMARY

In summary, some of the teachable principles horses can offer humans include:

- Horses have a low tolerance for inauthenticity and withholding the truth and will respond aggressively.

- Horses are non-judgmental and thus encourage us to be less judgmental of ourselves and others.

- Horses listen to what is happening on the inside of a person, not to the words a person says.

- Horses reveal the inner landscape of the human, including limiting beliefs, attitudes, and desire for change.

- Horse listens to the energy we are, our life force.

- Horses are unsentimental and resource efficient.

- Horses are predisposed to engage in relationship.

- Horses guide us into unknown, unexplored, and magical spaces of consciousness.

- Horses make decisions based on how they *feel*, not on how they *think*.

- Horses can teach us important concepts about roles in relationships that are not competitive, but rather cooperative.

- Horses can teach us to be more playful and curious with our change process.

- Horses remind us when we are not in the moment.

- The lead mare is the direction setter and is a rich metaphor for self-leadership.

- Horses depend on their intuitive and sensate feelings to determine safety vs. danger and to negotiate their position in relation to others (horse or human).

- Horses mirror the energy of our mood, tone, attitude, and intention.

- Predator-prey dynamics do not explain our long history with horses or EGE and should be avoided when explaining the power of EGE.

The Role of the EGE Facilitator

The Equine Guided Educator creates an experiential, supportive learning environment for participants to explore and create change in their lives. The unique component of EGE is the horse, of course. Thus, the Equine Guided Educator allows the horse to become the mirror of the inner landscape of the participant, comprised of unconscious and conscious interpretations and attitudes about his/her life – past, present, and future. Leveraging the process of "learning by doing" (experiential) integrated with the horse's natural wisdom and healing presence assists the facilitator in encouraging the participant to accept responsibility for his or her own learning and behavior.

EGE crosses many domains of the self-development process. People who seek an EGE facilitator are looking for assistance (whether through coaching or therapy) to navigate a change in their personal, professional, or fundamental (personal and professional) domains.

Some people seek a therapist with EGE training to understand their psychological dilemmas or to process past traumas. The horse in this case can act as a healer, allowing people to purge their feelings. When a person needs a good cry, the horse has a natural ability in opening the floodgates so the tears of pain or loss can be experienced and processed. Sometimes the horse becomes the mirror of the person's self-projections, which the therapist utilizes to gain information about the client's inner state of mind.

Some people hire a coach or mentor with EGE training to help them develop and articulate goals and ambitions or to navigate an important transition. This transition requires a process of exploration and planning. To make a transition and change our current trajectory often involves a process of inquiring about options and choices before deciding on a particular set of expected outcomes and actions required to accomplish these goals.

In this situation the horse offers a unique way to explore new ideas and open the mind's imagination. The horse mirrors the energetic quality of the old story versus the new story that wants to be created, helping both client and EGE facilitator to know when they are headed in a new direction towards the anticipated goal and when they are back in the old stories or patterns of relating.

In order to facilitate the EGE process, it is important for the facilitator to understand the process of creating and moving through change. She should also be well versed in basic human behavior and equine behavior concepts and patterns of interaction and relating. Ideally, she brings many years of professional competency in either (or both) the horse and human domains and partners with other professionals in the domains where they have limited experience.

New goals can include making a career transition or changing the dynamics in a relationship, such as divorce or loss of a loved one. Creating change can involve helping a leader embody the next level of leadership skill to grow the team and/or company. Other foci of the change process can include developing self-confidence, enhancing communication and coordination skills, staying focused on goals, learning how to be a better listener, developing compassion, and other relational skills.

The EGE facilitator allows the horse to *guide* the process of learning, reflecting, and exploring. She combines the process of kinesthetic learning and cognitive reflection in relation to the client's mental, physical, spiritual, emotional, and social well-being. Through the process of evaluating an individual's current patterns of behavior, perceptions, and performance, the Equine Guided Educator encourages the client towards a healthy self-image and supports the exploration of new practices for achieving personal and/or professional goals.

The Equine Guided Educator guides her clients through a learning process that is centered on their ambitions and goals for the future. She assists her clients in refining their gifts and creating environments in which they can thrive. She facilitates the client's growth and learning through experiential exercises with horses. The horse, in this process, literally guides the client

86

and the facilitator by revealing inner states of mind and physical energetic states of presence that are either enhancing or inhibiting a person's ability to effectively change and grow. Through the process of EGE, the facilitator cultivates the client's integration of mind, body, and spirit.

DEFINING YOUR DOMAIN OF COMPETENCY

The unique and profound opportunities that arise from bringing horses to people for the sake of growth and learning are both exciting and serious. When the emotions of the participants are incongruent with other energies within their environment, horses can become unpredictable in ways that even an experienced horse person cannot anticipate. While a person may be competent with horses and/or human development, incorporating the two requires a whole new set of competencies. The safety of the horse and human – emotionally, physically and spiritually – is an important and sensitive matter.

The EGE facilitator should be skilled and competent in a specific domain or domains. Examples of domains include horsemanship, leadership, personal development, women in transition, youth at risk, veterans, etc.

An Equine Guided Educator demonstrates through curriculum vitae and specific courses of study in EGE that she has studied to be a horse specialist, a human specialist, or both. An individual who does not already have extensive equine or human development skills should not expect to become competent to work with people and horses through attending any single EGE program.

A person who does not have experience with horses or human development needs to acquire additional learning in either the human or horse component. The EGE process can become intimate and personal even under superficial circumstances. By this, I mean that a horse-riding instructor with or without EGE experience may experience a student going into a triggered space or remembering a negative experience or harsh self-judgment that has historic roots. Since the horse-riding instructor is not a therapist or a coach, as long as the instructor keeps wearing the horsemanship hat and just listens, he or she stays within personal competency. But if, on the other hand, the instructor attempts to dialogue about the student's experience or draws external connections between the horse's current behavior and the student's other personal or professional life, then that instructor may be stepping outside of his or her domain of competence.

If the Equine Guided Educator is not a horse expert, then she needs to partner with someone who is. Because of the inherent risks involved with equine activities, it is essential that an experienced equine specialist be present at any process in which a student/client is near or around horses. Even with an equine specialist present, the Equine Guided Educator needs to have some experience with horses. She needs to be comfortable around horses and understand the basic safety issues associated with horses. Ideally, the equine specialist should also be trained as an Equine Guided Educator.

To make this amazing process accessible to the public, it is important that we collaborate and learn together to develop a consistent industry standard. It is also important to respect what experts in the field who are committed to developing this discourse have already learned. The more that we learn from each other and share our experiences, the more Equine Guided Education will develop and flourish as a respectable and important part of human learning and growth.

While some professionals may have extensive horsemanship and coaching skills, the EGE process creates a whole new paradigm for learning. While the EGE process is unique and profound, it can also be complex and unpredictable. A complete paradigm shift in consciousness and learning takes place. An EGE professional needs to be skilled in recognizing even the slightest shifts in states of mind and energetic responses in the horse, human, and environment at any given moment. It is essential to have experience or knowledge in the EGE process before attempting to facilitate the process.

Even professionals with extensive horsemanship skills must unlearn many of the horsemanship skills they have been taught in order for EGE to be successful.

MODELING THE PRINCIPLES OF EGE

As an EGE facilitator you are a role model for your clients. Your clients observe how you create an open, centered presence, how you listen, how you inquire, and how you interpret the communication between horse and human. They perceive your body language more than the words you say, even if they are not aware they are doing so. It is essential to embody the very practices and mood of exploration in which you are asking the client to participate.

One aspect that is truly unique to the EGE process is that the horse is not only mirroring the client, he is mirroring you as well. Thus it is very important for you as the EGE facilitator to embody the basic principles of self-reflection, somatic presencing, and self-awareness. It is important to have a deep understanding of your own nature and your strengths as well as your limiting patterns. It is important for you to know the boundaries of your own competence in regards to horsemanship, human development, spiritual interpretation, and domains of learning.

When a coach or therapist is in the middle of personal inquiries and dilemmas it is far easier to put those aside when in an office or indoor workspace. Once the facilitator has included a horse in the process, the facilitator's need to be fully present to the client and not distracted by her own dilemma's is greatly increased. I have seen situations in which the EGE facilitator is not fully present and instead is carrying personal projections of the horse and/or the human into the EGE session.

In such a situation, the horse is actually mirroring the facilitator and not the client. If the facilitator fails to acknowledge that this is occurring, the facilitator is contaminating the client's process with the facilitator's own personal issues.

ATTRIBUTES OF AN EGE PROFESSIONAL

First and foremost to the EGE process is the facilitator's role in encouraging self-awareness and exploration from a non-linear perspective. The facilitator integrates multiple sources of information, not just logical thinking. Intuitive information is ever present in the EGE process and can be revealed in the form of pictures, images, sensations, energetic tone, and the potential collaboration of the other animals and local surroundings. Even the weather patterns can offer a unique reflection of the mysterious influence of unconscious, intuitive perceptions.

Next comes the ability to imagine and explore, which requires curiosity and openness to different interpretations. While creating a space of inquiry, the facilitator stays focused on the client's articulated goals and does not get lost in the storyline or in over-processing through our traditional rational conversations.

The EGE facilitator needs to stay present and focused without becoming consumed by performance anxiety ("How am I doing?"), or her own agenda of what should be happening ("We planned to do 'xyz,' therefore we should stick with it"). At the same time, the EGE facilitator avoids creating bias ("I know what the client really needs or wants") and instead embodies an *anything is possible* attitude.

The EGE facilitator understands the importance that *body memory* plays in healing and focuses on creating new and more positive attitudes and behaviors from a somatic perspective. What I mean here is that it is not enough to just change one's story or mental perspective. The client must also practice changing the way his or her animal body responds and reacts to change. The facilitator plays an important role in helping the client develop these new practices.

The facilitator demonstrates active listening, compassion, and freedom of thought. The facilitator embodies the same non-judgmental presence that the horse offers.

Paramount to creating a sustainable platform for growth and change is the facilitator's ability to navigate between the patterns of the logical mind and the intuitive spirit that is naturally a part of being human. To do this well requires an understanding of time and space and the likely possibility that intentions (whether conscious or unconscious) are the driving force behind change, like the fuel that makes the engine run in a car. The fuel that drives the car came from the belly of the earth, ancient in its experience of time and space.

Therefore, the facilitator should have some understanding of the influence of time – past, present, and future – and the consequential tension between *living in the moment*, acknowledging the past, and nurturing the future.

TRANSLATING THE HORSE'S RESPONSES

The Equine Guided Educator understands the importance of allowing the horse to become the primary guide in this unique and unusual process. The more a facilitator can allow the horse to do the *work of guiding*, the more the facilitator can allow clients to create their own insights and conclusions. To me, this is at the heart of any great facilitation process: allowing clients to come up with their own discoveries and create their own practices for change. It takes great skill for the facilitator to back away from her own or her client's expectation that the facilitator will do most of the work. The inherent gift in having the horses as part of the change process is that if the facilitator can transfer the emphasis of the inquiry through a conversation and relationship with the horse, many of our human foibles around change can be avoided. In addition, the issues of transference and projection can be minimized.

Further, the Equine Guided Educator needs to develop the skill of translating the horse's feedback in such a way that the client can receive this often intense feedback as a form of support. Leveraging the process of *learning by doing* integrated with the horse's natural wisdom and healing presence, the EGE facilitator encourages clients to accept responsibility for their own learning and behavior. When clients can create their own insights and realizations through their engagement with the horse, their likelihood of creating sustainable change is dramatically increased. This is distinct from a coach who offers too much advice, suggestion, or input during the early phases of the change process.

In order to translate the horse's response effectively, the facilitator must believe that the horse is an actual mirror. The facilitator needs to interpret the horse's body language in an open-ended way that does not include overly exaggerated interpretations commonly found in the human desire to create meaning. This requires training. People from all walks of life tend to rush into human interpretations of animal behavior without fully understanding the biological nature of the animal. This can actually create a rich dialogue in our human conversations in which we can learn to observe without projection.

Observing without projection can give us vital information about the nuances of our interpretations and the underlying stories that formulate our projections. This is a unique feature of EGE work: Since the horse is an animal that people are compelled by, yet they do not actually know what the horse is thinking and feeling, they come to realize that their story of what the horse is thinking or feeling is actually their own. The EGE facilitator navigates this opportunity and turns it into a self-reflective process in order to gain more insights into the clients' schemas and attitudes.

In this process the facilitator encourages the client to explore different interpretations, which can lead to new stories about historic events and create new stories about the future. In addition, the facilitator guides the client to discern between trivial dialogues versus significant issues, and seeks to focus only on relevant issues. The facilitator also makes note and reflects back to the client when the client has fallen back into old stories that are no longer effective and are inhibiting the process of change.

It is natural for facilitators to have their own projections and interpretations. The art of facilitation is to notice these without forming an attachment to them or fixing them as real or *the truth*. This skill takes years to develop. One of the advantages of having horses present in this process is that the facilitator is not only observing her own projections, while filtering them with the client's projections, but is adding the filter of the horse's behavior. The facilitator is asking herself, "Are the horse's reactions to the client matching my interpretations?" In this way the horse acts as a *reality check* for both facilitator and client.

SUMMARY

The EGE facilitator provides an environment where participants can:

- Cultivate and develop the "self" in relation to their current life and future goals

- Design and practice "who they are becoming"

- Reflect on their patterns of thought, behavior, and action

- Identify new skills and ways of thinking and responding to life

- Learn how to learn and appreciate the process of change

- Engage in experiential learning practices with fellow students

Effective learning occurs when a person engages in some activity, reflects upon the activity, derives useful insight from the analysis, and incorporates the result through a change in understanding and/or behavior. As Lao Tzu once said, "You cannot learn from a good book, because a book will not tell you what you do not want to hear." Some common learning schemas include:

- Identifying and developing ambitions and aspirations

- Developing the ability to stay focused on goals

- Enhancing communication and negotiation skills

- Encouraging self-confidence and self-esteem

- Developing trust of oneself and others

- Learning how to listen to and respect intuitive senses

- Building effective relationship and interactive practices

- Uncovering old stories and behaviors that are no longer effective

- Developing new stories and behaviors relevant to one's goals

- Developing one's leadership and management style

- Understanding and developing team dynamics

- Learn new ways of thinking, exploring, and imagining

The Process of Change

Why do people go to therapy or hire a coach? People choose to go to a therapist or a coach when they want to make a change in their lives. A desire for change can be precipitated by significant events such as the death of a loved one, losing a job, or starting or ending a relationship. Sometimes people are not sure why they want to seek counsel except that they feel as if something is missing in their lives or they are feeling frustrated but are not sure why.

A person who is seeking counsel often senses that he or she is facing a dilemma (the point of change) and does not feel confident to go through such a transition alone. The person may feel a need to dig deeper into the reason or desire for change in order to fully understand its significance and to consider the possible outcomes of choosing one solution over another. Others may seek counsel simply to improve the way they think about their lives, the way they navigate relationships and make decisions about their future.

It is natural for people to go through transitions throughout their lives. I notice that these transitional phases can be as frequent as every five to ten years. The most commonly recognized change points in one's development are the teenage years and the mid-life years, but often more subtle and just as important change points are occurring throughout one's life.

A person facing into a point of change may gracefully accept it as an adventurous project or see it as a terrifying, painful experience. The person may even flip flop between either extreme. Change itself brings with it a wide array of emotional responses: joy, fear, sadness, anger, excitement, doubt, confidence, confusion, indecision, stubbornness, guilt, shame, peace.

Having experienced numerous different therapists and self-development programs over the years, I have come to the opinion that many of these approaches have good intentions for assisting people through their points of change, but they miss the critical phase of integrating insight into new action. It is relatively easy to create an environment where the participant goes through a range of emotions, simply because change is scary and triggers emotional responses. And yet, moving through change requires more than emotional output. It requires new interpretations and new actions.

In the EGE process it is not only important to know what the person's specific issue or change point is, it is also important to know what phase of change the person is in in order to effectively design and implement appropriate equine guided activities. Different exercises with horses require different conversations and sets of actions that coincide with different phases of the learning and/or change process.

For the EGE professional, several factors need to be taken into consideration:

- Is the person coming to you on her/his own recognizance or is she/he part of a program in which participation with you is mandatory?

- Has the person identified a specific dilemma or point of change?

- What phase of change is the person in?

For people who are in a program such as a youth program, rehabilitation program, or leadership program in which they have not individually signed up for the EGE process, the process of creating a space for change can be more challenging. For example, some of these people may not feel that they need to change. They may not be ready or trusting enough to engage in the discomfort that comes with learning. In addition, group dynamics vary and each individual's level of readiness may be different, as may each individual's phase in the change process. This dilemma can become a complex negotiation for the EGE professional and will be discussed later in the chapter.

For now, let's begin by summarizing the phases of change and the typical types of conversations, explorations, and facilitation that occur in each phase. Diagram 1 shows the different phases of thinking and types of conversations associated with each phase of the change process. The change process can also be seen as the process of learning in general. In order to change, we need to learn new ways of thinking, new ways of perceiving, new ways of relating to our situations, and new actions and behaviors. You can work with this change chart for an individual, for a group of people, for a team, and for a business. This chart helps the EGE professional stay focused on the clients EGE process, exercises to offer and conversations to encourage or to move beyond. For instance once someone is really clear about their new direction, they need to be in conversations for action rather than only exploring new ideas.

Diagram 1: The Process of Change

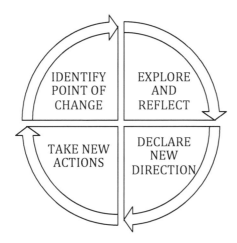

Phase 1: Identify Point of Change

- Acknowledge and accept that change is happening

- Open into an inquiry with curiosity

- Identify domain of change

- Identify what is inhibiting change

- Determine what is missing, not working, or wanting to come to form

- Encourage and allow for new learning

Phase 2: Explore and Reflect Upon What You Care About

- Explore possibilities and choices

- Examine patterns of thought, beliefs, and behavior

- Evaluate values and ethics

- Distinguish between Old story vs. New story

- Develop new story of "who I am now"

- Explore alternative behaviors and practices

Phase 3: Make Declaration About New Story

- New focus on what is important

- New story of "who I am now"

- Articulate and commit to specific sets of actions

- Practice embodying new story

- Develop confidence and resilience

Phase 4: Take New Actions

- Establish and maintain new practices to support new direction

- Develop self-leadership

- Integrate oneself into larger social system

- Develop a relational self

ACKNOWLEDGING THE POINT OF CHANGE

The point of change process begins with declaring a breakdown. A breakdown does not have to be a negative thing. A breakdown could be a new opportunity such as a job promotion or a new relationship. A breakdown could also be an emotional response to a new situation or a change in circumstance. And it can be a difficult situation like the sudden death of a spouse, or a major health issue that has just been diagnosed. Sometimes the point of change begins with a sense that something is no longer working or flowing in a person's life. It could even be experienced as a low to high level of frustration of unknown origins. And it can be as intense as feel literally life threatening.

The first step in identifying the point of change is to determine the domain in which the change wants to happen. The specific domain of change may not be easily identified at the beginning of the change process. The person could simply be experiencing a feeling or longing that has no words or clear description, a feeling of restlessness or frustration that intensifies with time until the person can no longer avoid the discomfort. Whether the person clearly recognizes the domain of change or not, a change is being asked for. As the Equine Guided Educator, it is important for you to work with the client to identify the domain of change. Is there a lack of alignment of mind, body, and/or spirit?

ESTABLISHING THE DOMAIN OF CHANGE

What domain of change is the person in? Another way to ask this question is, what area of a person's life is being affected? The change can often be categorized as within either the personal or professional domain, or it can be fundamental in that the change required is relevant to both personal and professional domains. A fundamental change has consequences and/or benefits across multiple domains. A fundamental change often requires examining and evaluating one's concepts, self-perceptions, and interpretations of past and present situations.

Personal Domains of Change

Sometimes a person's domain of change is in a personal domain such as health, relationship, parenting, finances, living circumstances, or home and hearth. Questioning about lifestyle, where one lives, and how one lives is a personal and important inquiry. Breakdowns or gaps in how a person is managing or perceiving personal living situations and personal relationships fall within the personal domain. How a person is attending to personal well being, either mentally, spiritually or physically, is an important aspect of self-identity and self-care. The habits and patterns of daily living are important considerations worthy of evaluation and inquiry.

Professional Domains of Change

Examples of professional domains include career identity, education in specific areas of expertise, financial compensation, peer relationships, and specific competencies required in the workplace. An executive evaluating whether to accept a promotion that requires new skills and competencies may require a change in self-perception, career ambition, and specific practices to develop the new skills required to succeed. If the promotion requires moving to a new state, then the point of change may also require evaluating how it will affect the person's living situation and family dynamics, which makes the point of change relevant to both the personal and professional domains.

Fundamental Change

Fundamental change requires re-evaluating core beliefs and values about life, relationships, and self-identity. It is not always clear where to begin the conversation of change, in which case starting with the most immediate pain or stress point will tend to lead into the more panoramic conversations regarding one's core sense and purpose.

Once the domain of change and the core topics needing to be addressed are identified, the change process begins with a process of inquiry. Inquiry is the process in which one begins to explore not only what is not working in one's life, but also what new concepts want to come to form. In order for open inquiry to occur, one must combat the underlying stories and concepts that have been attempting to inhibit the change process. This phase of learning is what I call a *both and process*. A person has to both explore new goals and desires and at the same time evaluate what is old and no longer realistic.

During this phase, it is important to recognize what stories or beliefs are associated with the breakdown. These stories or beliefs are often buried in subconscious memories of our life experience and may even be embodied (in the body). Unless we spend part of the change process getting familiar with these *below-the-radar* stories and concepts about self and others, the new goals and expectations being developed will not be able to manifest in a sustainable way.

Many of the passive Equine Guided activities encourage a somatic exploration of what wants to come into form, allowing our inner desires and ambitions to come to the foreground and be entertained. At the same time, we are exploring how our patterns and habits (the old stories) are either helping or hindering our ability to move forward into that future. In order to fully engage in this phase of inquiry one has to bring forward both curiosity and imagination. This may sound easy enough, but often one's inner critic or self-judgments attempt to hinder this process.

It is important for the EGE facilitator to understand how fear can be the significant driving factor in limiting a person's ability to move forward in life. Fear is a biological response, an actual physical, pre-cognitive response to external stimuli. Fear can arise without a person being conscious that the somatic, animal body is actually in a fear response. The concepts of fear will be addressed in the following chapter.

101

PHASE 2: EXPLORATION AND REFLECTION

Beginning the phase of exploration and reflection is part of the *both and process* I mentioned earlier. By this, I mean that it is not enough to focus merely on designing our future and creating new plans and outcomes. We also need to examine how our historical experiences and our subsequent interpretations of those experiences may be limiting our ability to move forward with new actions.

During this phase, we notice specific patterns in how we process information, the interpretations that we tend to make, and details about how we respond under pressure. The EGE facilitator during this phase is looking for repeating patterns. For example, the client may be in a different exercise with a different horse and yet the same bodily response and mental interpretation happens. The EGE facilitator may notice specific words that stand out as significant. He/she may notice the client's body expression repeating specific movements, like shallow breathing or arms folded over the chest. The facilitator may notice an incongruity between the words the client is saying and the body presentation or mood associated with the conversation.

This phase of change is also a time to re-evaluate the client's core values, ethics, and beliefs about life. In a sense, the EGE facilitator is providing a space to throw the client's cards in the air and see what falls in place. During this phase, client's stories and beliefs about their lives will come to the surface. Each one is evaluated to see if the clients still hold these concepts as valuable in the new stories they are creating about who they are and the future they are designing. Also under examination are the similarities and differences between the client's beliefs, ethics, and values, and those of the people with whom the client is in relationship (whether personal or professional).

It is important during this phase for the EGE professional to encourage the client to focus on his or her own self-evaluation as opposed to focusing on what is best for others. How the client needs to relate and interact with others comes later in the phase of change. In this phase, it is a personal quest to re-connect to one's core intentions or life purpose. Common inquiries include:

- Who am I as distinct from others?

- What am I naturally good at?

- What do I care about?

- What are my core values and beliefs about life, people, and relationships?

- What am I willing to do to make my vision happen?

- What am I not willing to do to make my vision happen?

- What offends me?

- Why is my vision important to me?

- What will it take for me to make this change?

- Where and to whom do I want to make a contribution?

- What stories and beliefs no longer serve me?

- Who I am becoming?

Once clients have re-connected to their core selves and sense of purpose, the next phase of exploration can be to inquire into how *the who they are* integrates into the world of others and the greater good. Common inquiries include:

- Who are the kind of people and community I want to be part of?

- What people are important to me?

- What kind of relationship do I want to have with them?

- What is the best way for me to contribute the best parts of myself?

- Who will benefit from my vision and why?

- What will be different in the world with this change?

- How will I know when I am succeeding in my change process?

- How will I know if I am successful at carrying out my vision?

- How do I want others to see me?

PHASE 3: MAKING DECLARATIONS

Once the client has gained clarity on his or her new direction and goals for the future, the EGE process moves into active exercises in which the participant makes a declaration about his or her new direction.

A declaration is a commitment to create a particular future paradigm. Making a declaration about one's desired goals and the specific outcomes that they will produce galvanizes one's intentions and becomes the focal point of future actions. Once a commitment is made to a specific series of outcomes, the EGE facilitator and the participant engage in designing and practicing what is required for the participant to embody the actions required to make his or her future happen as he or she intends it to.

The most basic declarations begin with "I am" statements. "I am a woman." "I am a mother." A person's declarations reflect the individual's identity, purpose, and stand in life. Another way to develop a declaration is with statements like, "I am a stand for living a sustainable lifestyle."

For example, Martin Luther King declared a future in which black people and white people would be able to share the same rights together. During his life, that future did not exist, but he believed in his vision with so much conviction that other people started to see the future he declared and began to change their intent and actions. In addition, his belief and embodiment of his declaration was so powerful that not a person in America was unsure of how he or she felt about his declaration. No one said, "I am not sure what I think of Martin Luther King." Rather, the power of his declaration inspired either a desire to engage in his vision or to act against it. Thus a powerful declaration engages others either to partake and support the potential future possibility or to decline to participate.

Because of the inherent potency of a declaration, some participants resist taking a stand for themselves and what they believe out of fear of what others will think. This phenomenon triggers our social instinct to be accepted by others. On one hand, if a participant does not take a stand for himself or herself and what he or she believes in, that person's spirit may begin to wither and fear will inhibit his or her ability to live the life he or she is destined to live, further limiting that person's ability to fully contribute his or her unique outlook and approach to life. On the other hand, finding the courage to be one's unique self and to make the contribution that is one's own to make allows amazing new accomplishments in terms of self-identity, self-worth, and greater contributions to the world. In addition, a person who takes a stand and embodies his or her own beliefs provides inspiration and clarity to others.

A declaration is not fixed in stone. Sometimes the participant practices making a specific declaration only to find a need to change a few elements to make it more authentic to the desired outcome. It is through practice that participants develop the confidence and deeper belief in their goals that is required to overcome self-doubt and fear.

PHASE 4: TAKING NEW ACTIONS

In order to actually accomplish new goals and paradigms, we need to not only to change the way we think and articulate our life path, we also need to embody our vision through the actions we take. Taking action includes how we negotiate with others, how we engage others in our vision, how we respond to unexpected setbacks, etc. It includes our daily practices required to stay healthy in mind, body, and spirit.

New actions can be as simple as following up on a plan of action, the actual requests and offers we need to make to incorporate our vision into a reality. New actions can include calling a loved one on a consistent basis, or taking a walk in nature every day.

Taking new actions is one of the most important components of actually following through on one's objectives. Taking new actions is about practice. Remember the old saying, "You cannot learn how to swim by reading a book about swimming." Recurrent practice and focus on what specific actions are required is the predominant focus of this phase of change.

Regular review and analysis of progress being made is also a valuable and important component of this phase. The EGE facilitator can assist the participant in reviewing what new actions have been embodied, in the sense that the participant is now able to be self-generating in these actions. This means that the participant is able to sustain the change in thought and action on his or her own. Review and analysis of progress can identify new areas for the participant to develop.

SUMMARY

Encouraging imagination and creative thinking is important in every phase of the change process. Open exploration allows the possibility to reinterpret the past and historic events and at the same time permits new discovery and a new intention to follow.

Identify and Evaluate Patterns and Habits

- Get support from external observers like the horses, a coach, the EGE facilitator and/or other participants.

- Be a learner and allow yourself be coachable.

- Intensify your self-reflection and inquiry.

- Avoid falling into judgment especially during learning because it closes possibilities and shuts down new ways of exploring opportunities.

- Investigate and explore biological instincts for clues to how we respond to life. We are animals first, with universal concerns for survival. One of our primary instincts is *to be of value* and to contribute to the greater good.

- Our body responds to the environment first. Our mental process is secondary, and often inaccurate.

- Learn and be able to identify your instinctive *"automatic response under pressure"*: Appease: Get close for safety, be overly nice, appeasing, smile and laugh even when uncomfortable. Flight: Fade into background for safety, be overly quiet, avoid conflict, and emotionally disappear in conflict. Fight: Fight or become argumentative when uncomfortable or challenged; become defensive, challenging, and/or judgmental.

- Focus on your core priorities through inquiry and discussion. Practice asking, *"What are my choices"* vs. just reacting.

- Develop intuitive listening and sensate responses. Observe pre-cognitive impressions. Intuition does not have an agenda. It is hard to articulate in words.

    It is more like a feeling. We don't think intuition; it arises spontaneously. Distinct from paranoia, intuition does not have a storyline.

Exploration and Reflection

- Reinterpret the past and historic events.

- Change the way you perceive yourself, others, and the world. Develop new stories about the future and how you want to be.

- Create new choices in how to react to pressure, stress, and conflict.

- Develop stronger relationships with people.

- Increase your capacity to communicate and coordinate without emotional baggage.

- Increase your ability to observe others who may be reactive and resistant.

- Develop compassion for yourself and for others.

Self-Development Principles

We are our biology. We are animal beings. We embody our deeper concepts of self-identity, which can be either healthy or unhealthy interpretations of who we are and how others see us. As animals, we sense others, we smell them. We feel their energy. How people *are* (their *way of being*) influences how we think of them and whether we want to connect with them or avoid them.

Others feel us in much the same way. We think we walk around hiding ourselves from others. Quite the contrary, we are big sandwich board signs. When I first start working with people they think they cannot interpret others well or see subtle displays of energy. But I have come to learn that we all have a keen ability to read the subtle, underlying perceptions of others. We are much more accurate than we think we are. In fact, we are doing it all the time. The problem is that we are not always aware that we are interpreting others, all the time, from the animal part of us.

Humans and horses are inspired by a person's *presence*. A person who has presence is authentic in that inner thoughts and energy match external presentation. A person with presence also has an expanded awareness of herself in relation to others. She is in choice. She chooses how she thinks, acts, and relates to the collective herd that she has chosen to be part of. She follows her path without self-doubt, embraces appropriate social boundaries, and integrates herself with the various personality styles of the group.

Horses know when we are being present because we are centered and focused on what is important to us, while at the same time demonstrating flexibility and openness to change. When we are centered on what we care about, we are balanced in the four dimensions of mental, physical, emotional, and spiritual awareness.

In contrast, when we are off-center, we are triggered into automatic responses, reactions, and judgments.

109

THE PRINCIPLES OF PRESENCE

- Somatically embodied

- Authentic expression – body language and energetic tone match the words spoken

- Open to other perspectives rather than being rigid

- Curious and creative

- Connected to your core values

- Connected to your body's experience and your senses

- Present to others and the environment

- Focused on what you care about

- Observes situations from different perspectives

- Listens to others' points of view

- Tolerates uncertainty or conflict

- Refrains from judgmental thinking of self and others

- Able to build trust with others

For example, in personal relationships, a person who practices staying centered is genuinely open to the interpretations of others without feeling a need to agree or disagree. In a present state of mind, we accept the possibility that others may see things differently than we do. We are focused on our desired outcome and do not get swept into the drama or the emotional aspects of the dilemmas or issues in front of us. Rather than reacting, we are aware that we have many choices of how to respond to the situation.

On the other hand, when a person is off-center, he or she is triggered by emotions and gripped by reactive feelings. This outlook tends to spiral further into an off centered presence where the focus is on changing the 'other' rather than staying centered on one's own presence.

SELF-REFLECTION

Self-reflection is essential to improving our capacity to act effectively in our lives and work. To be open to the strengths and limitations of our persona, we must understand that we are an integral part of our own successes and failures. Distinct from self-assessments and the assessments of others, self-reflection is a process of reviewing the consequences of one's behavior and actions. Self-reflection is not an automatic process and some individuals are naturally more inclined towards self-reflection than others.

What we pay attention to comes to the foreground of our awareness. We may become aware that we are breathing in short, quick breaths. Through reflecting on the consequences of not breathing deeply we may determine that we have constricted our experience, causing a contraction in our body, mind or spirit. We may then focus our attention on breathing deeply and thus allowing our bodily sensations to become more transparent and part of our actual experience and response.

Another example of self-reflection is when a rider notices that her horse has become jittery and nervous. Through her self-reflection she becomes aware that her hands are tightly holding onto the reins and pulling too steadily on the horse's mouth, causing the horse discomfort. Following her new awareness, she relaxes her hands and loosens her grip on the reins, and the horse relaxes in response.

Self-reflection can be as simple as noticing our state of mind and body language in current time, or it can occur through reviewing past experiences and looking for repeating patterns and stories.

At some point in our self-reflection practices, we may allow another being (that we trust) or the environment to provide us with feedback that may be different than our own experience and become curious how our behavior and body language is influencing creating a similar or different response.

Effective self-reflection can occur in EGE when both the client and the facilitator allow the possibility that the horse's actions are a direct response to the client's words and actions as well as underlying attitudes and energetic sensations of the particular topic being explored.

Horses in the EGE process provide a powerful reflection of how we show up somatically and the effect we have on others in our lives. They reflect our mood – are we happy, angry, afraid, timid, relaxed, centered? Are we communicating clearly? Do we believe ourselves? Do we have a body, a self, that is going to take us in the direction we want to go, or are there incongruities present? When we are open to this feedback, we can self-reflect and recognize how our automatic way of communicating affects our lives and those around us. We can listen more deeply to ourselves and others. We can practice new ways of interacting with the world that are more aligned with our ambitions.

SELF-RESPONSIBILITY

Self-responsibility is a form of leadership. Leadership is a form of relationship: how I am leading myself in relation to my inner calling, in relation to the others in my life, and in relation to my values about life.

On a personal level, leadership is about how we lead our own lives. Are we attending to our concerns and taking actions to make our lives turn out, or are we letting life happen to us? Are we living in a static state of complacency, or are we directing ourselves into the future? It's not enough to deserve a good life, we earn it.

To be a leader of our lives, we declare a goal, hold the commitment to the goal, create the intention and vision required to reach the goal, listen to the concerns of those relevant to the goal (in this case, the horse), make promises and declarations about the goal, and take care of breakdowns along the way.

In our leadership practice with horses, the horse reflects back to us the importance of embodiment. Horses expect us to embody what we care about, to believe in our ambitions. They ask us what we are centered on. They ask us to be accountable for not only our own performance but also on performance of the team as a whole (which includes them). They reflect back to us, moment by moment, how effectively, or not, we are leading them. When the horse does not do what we are asking of it, 95% of the time it is because we are not clearly communicating or are completely absorbed in negative self-assessments. Such moments are opportunities for us to examine our leadership and how we are failing to communicate. Are we presenting our vision clearly? Is our mood off? Are we sending mixed cues? Do we believe that what we are asking is attainable? Are we committed to our goals?

360 AWARENESS

The horse is keenly aware of its surroundings. Even a duck flying off the pond can become, for an instant, a perceived threat to the horse's survival. Some horses flee before thinking, and after gaining distance, may have the state of mind to turn back and actually look at what scared them.

One of the major causes of injury to equestrians is falling off of a spooked horse. The more the equestrian is able to foresee potential spooky objects or situations, the more likely the rider will stay on when the horse starts to flee. So it is imperative for a rider's safety to develop the ability to sense subtle changes in noise, movement, shadow, and light.

In order to do this well, the equestrian has to be in her feeling body, not her thinking body. Her awareness of her surroundings and her horse has to be at one hundred percent every moment. She has to sense what she cannot see. Horses can see farther, hear more, and smell things we can't even imagine.

In the self-development process the metaphor of having 360-degree awareness translates into a person's ability to step into a feeling state and listen to what is not spoken. It also translates into the ability to maintain peripheral vision and focused vision at the same time. This means being able to stay focused on the big picture (one's desired outcome), as well as focused on the task at hand.

Case Study

Emily was a massage therapist who was working with me to grow her small business. When she worked with the horse, she would look right at the horse's head and lose all context of her surroundings, let alone the horse's body. When she rode the horse she would look down through the horse's ears at the ground. The horse would lower its head in response and plug along. Her actions with the horse directly translated to how she was in her life in general. She lived in the moment; she had no future plan for herself or her business. She was at the whim of the wind, so to speak.

During her lessons I had her practice developing a peripheral view, meaning seeing her business in a longer perspective of time. When she rode, I had her practice looking twenty feet in front of the horse, rather than down at the ground. This helped her to develop forward thinking.

When she noticed that she was looking at the horse's ears, she would put her attention and focus on the bigger picture, the horizon. Over the next few months she successfully completed a marketing strategy and client-per-week goals. She continued to practice paying attention to the whole of her business rather than just the day-to-day details.

The practice of peripheral vision when around horses is not only practical; it translates to developing a plan of action for the future and staying focused on the desired outcome.

LISTENING

The conversation about intuition or sensing leads into the distinction of listening. When we are working in relationships or in teams, what we think of ourselves or how we are doing is less important than how those we engage with respond to us. Do they fulfill our requests begrudgingly or do they respond to our requests with a sense of pleasure? Working with horses, we build a sensitivity, a capacity for listening to how they respond to our requests and our declarations. Their listening to us will tell us more about how we are showing up than our own personal assessments.

The horse's feedback of our leadership is direct and immediate. They mirror how we appear to them. Quite often this is how we appear to other people in our everyday lives, in our relationships, and in our professions. It is often easier to accept the horse's assessments of us than those of our colleagues and loved ones because we know that the horse has no psychological agenda with us. We can't negate the horse's feedback by saying it is jealous or pissed off at us. The clear feedback of horses offers us new challenges and opportunities for improving our presence.

To listen to another's concerns is to offer the possibility of building trust and intimacy. It allows the other's concerns to be as legitimate as our own. With horses, the name of the game is listening and honoring the horse as a legitimate partner in the team. If we pay attention only to our concerns, we will not hear that our signals may not be working for the horse or that danger is ahead. With horses, the listening is subtle, since we cannot talk about the breakdown or ask what is wrong; we intuit through the sensations of our body and the horse's body. By learning to read moods and attitudes through the eye of the horse, we are also learning how to listen more deeply and accurately to other people's non-verbal communication. We listen and respond to that which is not spoken. When the mood is off, we can guide the conversation back to a shared center of concerns where we can re-connect the team to its shared purpose.

OPEN MIND

To move into this other landscape where horses become healers and teachers, we have to have an open mind complete with the sunrise and sunset of our imagination. When we have that kind of open mind, stories, images, different things will come in, overriding the rational interpretations that tend to misinterpret and clog the creative vessels of learning.

Open mind means no judgments. Any stories that begin with, "I should . . . " are not open-minded conversations. They are probably old stories created either by the client or by someone else in the client's life, most commonly a parent figure. The EGE facilitator encourages putting the *shoulds* aside in favor of open-minded inquiry.

AUTHENTICITY

The horse's willingness to trust the human arises out of its keen ability to perceive the human's authenticity, silently measuring the coherence between inner thought and outer expression. The horse perceives what is actually happening inside the human and mirrors this internal reality. The horse does not listen to our words, our convincing tone or smiling face. It listens only to that part of us that is authentic, that is naturally inside of us at that moment.

Because horses are so sensitive to our inner emotions, authentic conversations become the norm in the EGE process. Horses teach us how to respect our inner feelings without blame and judgment. They teach us how to be honest and in integrity with our deeper authentic conversation, because they consistently point out when we are not being honest. They demand our authenticity. When we are inauthentic with the horse, problems become apparent immediately. The following story illustrates how sensitive horses are to our inner thoughts and fears.

I'm Okay, No I'm Not

The minute Jane came into the round pen, Mimi, a petite white mare, became agitated. Her usually quiet and sweet demeanor turned into a mass of anxiety. She began pushing against Jane aggressively, trying to toss her off balance. I moved in between Mimi and Jane – creating some distance between them. Mimi, still agitated, rubbed her neck on the fence like she was trying to rub off a burr embedded in her skin and she paced back and forth nervously. I stepped Mimi away from Jane several more feet and she began to calm down.

"So, talk to me," I said.

Jane replied, "I don't know what is going on."

"Mimi is responding to an unacknowledged, intense energy and feels a need to get rid of it. If she is responding to something inside of you – perhaps some unacknowledged energy – what do you think she is reflecting about you?" I asked.

"I don't know. It can't be what I think it is," she muttered as tears began to stream down her face. She tried to hold her breath to no avail. And as her body demanded air, she finally screamed in a raw guttural voice, "I am terrified that my husband is going to leave me! My first husband left the children and me. I was devastated and I can't get over this fear that it is going to happen to me again."

"Has your current husband threatened to leave you?"

"No, he is wonderful. I don't know why I am so afraid." Jane wept. "I am so angry. Do you think that is why Mimi is so upset?"

"Jane, she could be mirroring your internal angst and unresolved anger about your original loss," I gently suggested.

A few moments passed and I drew her attention back to the horse, "Notice that since you have become more authentic, and you have acknowledged your inner thoughts, Mimi has settled down."

Mimi's dramatic response to Jane facilitated Jane's acceptance of this intense residual fear. It was no longer okay to keep it buried inside and pretend she was fine. She needed to deal with her past and look into the present to determine if history would repeat itself or if she was being driven by the fear of abandonment that her physical body still held as a *true story*. She further realized that if she did not become responsible for her fear and anxiety she could very well create a self-fulfilling prophecy of rejection.

Jane had been able to fool herself and her therapist into believing that she had healed from being abandoned by her first husband. The horse, however, felt the unresolved trauma. If the horse could feel her inauthenticity, she realized that her children probably also felt it. She decided to continue working on this new insight so that her children would not have to take on her inner emotional state as Mimi had done.

Authenticity is expressed by a *genuine congruence* between the inner and outer emotional, energetic states of being. Jane's experience with the horses revealed that her inner emotional state did not match her outer emotional expression. Her internal and external stories were in conflict. During the EGE process, the horse had a strong reaction to her inauthenticity. Horses are unwilling to accept our false pretenses. They only listen to what is on the inside. When our inner and outer presentations are incongruent, the horse enters a state of agitation.

When horses react to a person who is being inauthentic it is as though they are offended that this person is not being responsible for himself or herself. Being a social animal that knows – with every ounce of its body – that the survivability of the whole depends on each individual's capacity to be self-responsible, the horse is irritated by the inauthentic human's lack of self-responsibility.

Even though we cannot say for sure what the horse is thinking, we can assume that the horse is calling out *the elephant in the room*. The person's incongruence creates danger for the group as a whole and to other individuals. Rather than just fleeing the situation, the horse becomes increasingly aggressive toward the incongruent person as if to remove them from their space. I often wonder if the dramatic displays of aggression in these situations are the horse's attempt to shout out, *"Don't lie to me. It's not safe!"*

Over the years I have experienced far more aggressive responses to inauthenticity in group situations and private sessions. I have learned to sense the energy of individuals in a learning group at the beginning of the program. If I begin to feel agitated, or tense, I am on the alert for inauthenticity. It is necessary for me to be hyper-alert, because I don't want to risk either the people's or the horses' well being – physical, emotional, or spiritual – by putting that person in close proximity to horses.

I have even had horses begin to race around the arena for no apparent reason when a new group arrives and no one is even in the arena with them. Sure enough, there is a person in the group who is not being self-responsible and instead is blaming others, while at the same time smiling and pretending to be engaged with the group. The horse's intense response to someone who may be more than fifty feet away is quite astounding and *commands respect*. In these situations, I address the issue before people are allowed to approach the horse.

While this kind situation is rare, it is one very important reason why people need to carefully train and learn how to do this work rather than winging it on their own.

Addressing Fear

Inauthentic or incongruent expressions are often masking a deep fear response. By this I mean that a biological fear response is felt in the body while the person is pretending to feel normal. Fear is instinctive. Fear inhibits learning and creating positive change in one's life. It is almost impossible to avoid addressing fear when you offer self-development programs or counseling with horses. Being prepared to address fear in 1 on 1 sessions and/or group programs is paramount to doing EGE work. Why? Because of the horse's response to the energy that is associated with fear and also because of how they respond to inauthentic expression as discussed in the last chapter.

Since horses mirror the energy and underlying attitudes of the surrounding humans, they too become afraid. Horses that become afraid become dangerous.

Fear is defined as an unpleasant emotion caused by the belief that someone or something is dangerous or life threatening. Fear can lead to feelings of anxiety concerning a potential outcome that may be perceived as uncomfortable or painful. Fear response is deep and instinctive. All animals have an innate fear associated with the drive for survival that exists before logic or rational thought. Fear is a bodily response triggered by bodily sensations and subsequently followed by perceptions of fear, i.e., stories about "why someone should be fearful."

Fear is often generated by unconscious associations between past events or external stimuli and current moments of experience. The body's visceral response to sights, sounds, smells, and other somatic stimuli can trigger an imagined return or re-occurrence of past events in which a similar set of stimuli was involved. For example, a person with an abusive father who would raise his voice and stretch his neck and head when angry would grow into adulthood and be fearful of people who demonstrated a similar display of authoritative dominance.

A scientific experiment designed to study fear tracked a woman who had lost her short-term memory. Every day for three months she would come to visit the doctor. And on each visit they would shake hands and greet each other as if they had met for the first time. After three months, the doctor put a tack in his hand and when she shook his hand the tack pricked her and her arm drew back in pain. The following day she would not shake the doctor's hand. She did not remember why, but her body memory did. This is a great example of how fear can be held or get stuck in the body.

A common and significant fear for survival can be triggered by our instinct as a social animal to be part of a group. Once this fear is present it can stimulate unconscious or conscious fear of being excommunicated, separated, not included, abandoned, or rejected.

The topic of fear is broad and essential. I speak more on fear as a biological phenomenon in my book, *Horse Sense for the Leader Within.* For now, what we need to know is that if fear is prevalent it will inhibit learning and prevent the process of change. Unexamined fear can collapse into judgments and moods that shut down the learning process. When a person is gripped by fear and judgment, exploring new interpretations and new paradigms is impossible. Fear and judgment are like stop signs, keeping us stuck in the past and disallowing any forward momentum.

The fear response can be as simple as a somatic response to external stimuli, which can consist of increased heart rate and blood flow. The increase in the flow of chemicals can also be seen as an increase in the energy streaming through the body.

Our animal body responds to environmental and external stimuli with a certain automaticity, which happens before our cognitive mind even has a chance to interpret what may actually be happening. The body responds first and the mind comes along after the fact and makes up an interpretation of the body's experience. It is precisely in this shift from bodily

122

experience to mental interpretation that many of our limitations arise.

The human quickly rushes to explain, understand, categorize, and rationalize its somatic or animal body's change in energy streaming through the body. These interpretations can become embedded in the subconscious and can ultimately close one's sense of possibility or ability to reach for new opportunities.

Visual stimuli, sounds, smells, and other physical sensations can trigger a person's somatic or bodily memory of a bad experience. The actual events occurring in present time may not even be related to past events. As in the example above, an authoritative facilitator can trigger a participant's memory of an abusive father. The participant may not be consciously aware that he is being triggered into a past memory, and in the moment may begin to shut down or defend himself against the facilitator and thus miss the opportunity to evaluate his response and be open to change. When this happens, it is important to attempt to distinguish between paranoid and unrealistic interpretations of self and others (the old story) and to focus one's attention on the new story wanting to come to form.

Diagram 2: Unexamined fears can stop learning and change

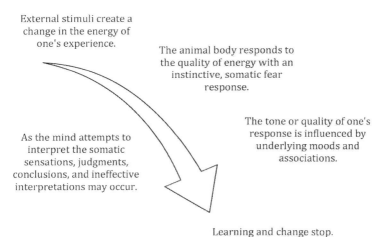

External stimuli create a change in the energy of one's experience.

The animal body responds to the quality of energy with an instinctive, somatic fear response.

As the mind attempts to interpret the somatic sensations, judgments, conclusions, and ineffective interpretations may occur.

The tone or quality of one's response is influenced by underlying moods and associations.

Learning and change stop.

When the fear response is followed by judgments, change is perceived as a bad idea. To change requires uncomfortable conversations and facing into what is not working in one's life. The fear and discomfort can become overwhelming, even if the discomfort is a natural part of changing one's perception of what is happening in current time as opposed to an uncomfortable memory of a historic event.

In order to move through change effectively, an evaluation of our fear response and our interpretation of it becomes part of the learning process. Evaluating the stories a person has about past events can be examined and the possibility for re-interpretation of past events and or the present situation can be discovered. In addition, uncovering the quality or mood of the story provides valuable information to further uncover the unconscious judgments.

It is important during this phase to engage "external observers" who can offer their experience of the current moment and somatic interpretations of the horse's response as it relates to the person's actions and body language. The horse in the EGE process is considered the primary and most important external observer. The facilitator is also an external observer whose role is to ask inquisitive questions during the EGE experience, followed by assessments relating to when the participant has collapsed into old stories or ineffective body language that is inhibiting the change towards new stories and body language. Other participants are also considered external observers, even though their reflections may be more or less helpful than the expertise of the facilitator and the straightforwardness of the horse.

FEAR CAUSES CONSTRICTION OF LIFE FORCE

Our life force, the energy comprised of our living system, runs up and down our blood stream. When a person shrinks away from life, or contracts from the core of his experience, he or she literally constricts the life force within. The physical constriction is held in the body and can be identified along what can be thought of as horizontal bands, as seen in diagram 3 on the next page.

This energetic contraction is like a rubber band, cutting off the core life force, creating a block. This block constricts the energy from flowing freely, thus causing a build-up of the energy, like blowing a balloon up with air until it wants to pop.

Horses are very sensitive to energy blocks or pent-up energy. If they are free to move around, they may release that energy by releasing tension in one of the areas shown in the diagram. For example, if a client has blocked energy in the throat region, resulting in an inability to speak freely or voice deeper emotions, the horse may yawn excessively in that person's presence. The EGE facilitator makes a note of this and may become more curious about the throat and how it may be the somatic indicator, the physical part of the body that is holding the old stories and judgments. If an EGE facilitator is trained to work somatically, she will connect the historic patterns of thought with the physical constriction and have the client emulate the horse's actions in order to release the energy.

Diagram 3: Constriction of Life Force

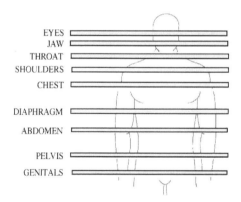

EYES
JAW
THROAT
SHOULDERS
CHEST
DIAPHRAGM
ABDOMEN
PELVIS
GENITALS

Horses mirror where tension or blocked energy resides in a person's body. They tend to be hypersensitive to such energetic bottling up or withholding, and become anxious or aggressive. The horse may simply become more nervous or jittery. In extreme expressions, the horse may even become aggressive towards other horses or the person who is experiencing these rigid stances.

I have even witnessed horses identifying areas of a client's body where there is an illness (past or present) that has created a chronic contraction of the life force. For example, one client of mine had a stomach ulcer and the horse she was working with kept biting at his belly in a hard, intense way. Through the course of five weeks, her ulcer cleared and she no longer had to be on medication.

At first I used to think that horses were at the very least showing us where the tension was residing, but now I wonder if they are actually helping the person release the energy, even if the person doesn't emulate the horse's actions or have an awareness of what is happening. The horse seems to have a magical ability to move and transfer energy, releasing blocked energy like virtual acupressure. Over the last twenty years, I have heard so many stories of people who felt that a specific constriction and/or associated story no longer held their attention after being with the horses. Once the energy was released from the body, the associated story had no more energy, no more life.

Constrictions of the life force are conditioned responses coupled with underlying moods and attitudes about life. They correlate to specific stories a person has that have become fixed, or rigid. These stories are actually judgments or conclusions about the self or others. Chronic constrictions in the body are often associated with traumatic or historic events. The energy that arose during these events gets stuck or trapped in the physical body and spiritual lifeline. Significant events that create could be one-time experiences or a repetitive series of events.

An example of a repetitive conditioned response is a young woman who clenches her jaw every time her mother yells at her. She is trying to hold in her anger towards her mother, which creates a constriction of her life force at the area of her jaw and mouth. As she stuffs her anger, pressure builds like a carbonated soda ready to explode when the can is opened. Since the energy (labeled as anger) is not released, it continues to percolate. Whenever she is in a situation in which a person reminds her of her mother, she tenses her jaw and her whole body becomes stiff and rigid. People tell her she is an angry person. She doesn't think she is an angry person and does not understand why people say this about her. The problem is she does not realize that when she clenching her jaw and that it makes her look angry. Her physical body is just trying to protect itself from getting yelled out, which historically created a significant fear response in the little girl.

Her body reacts to subtle cues that trigger the historic memory of being attacked. It doesn't think. Her mind, her rational process, isn't even aware that her body is now contracting her life force within. The gap between how she thinks she is being and how others perceive her bothers her. She doesn't understand what is wrong or how to fix it. Realizing that there is something amiss, she goes to a somatic coach to work on her anger issues.

The coach identifies her clenched jaw and helps her to learn how to release the contraction. She learns that her body goes into a fear response when a person pinches their lips together, or raises their voice. She also learns when she clenches her jaw, it is as if she is bracing for a rageful attack. Her somatic response to clench her jaw and withhold her anger has been conditioned over many years. It takes practice and reminding from her coach to relax her jaw. She notices that when she relaxes her jaw, she is not afraid anymore and can realize that the person in front of her is not actually her mother and nothing bad is about to happen.

If she does not learn to relax her jaw, she will have an awareness of her anger, but may not be able to fully resolve it without working somatically. Horses are somatic wizards who can help facilitators learn more about the somatic conditioning of the body.

INEFFECTIVE ATTITUDES ACT AS ENEMIES TO LEARNING

Anxiety, paranoia, distrust, judgment, righteousness, resentment, anger, defensiveness, or feeling like a victim are just a few attitudes that inhibit learning. The energy of these attitudes correlates with the contraction or constriction in the soma (as mentioned above), which can be held in the mind, body, or spirit of a person or in a combination of all three. When a person is in one of these states of mind, not only is the person's life force being constricted, like a tourniquet limiting blood flow to the extremities and organs, the mental agility and ability to navigate new paradigms of thought and behavior are also significantly reduced.

Resignation, depression, and despair are also significant attitudes that inhibit change. When a person is living in one of these contracted energetic states there is an overwhelming feeling of isolation and dis-ease. Hope, or being open to new possibilities, new stories, or new outcomes, is almost impossible. The client may follow a story that says there is nothing she can do to change things and she may feel a sense of powerless to change her circumstances and experience.

These states are very difficult to change compared to the states in which energy is actually moving. In the presence of these low-energy states the horse will lack energy and appear dull or resigned. The horse may drag its hooves through the dirt when walking, emphasizing a "heavy" energy. Sometimes the horse will shed a tear. When the life force of a person is energetically zapped, the possibility of change is not present. The dilemma is how to regain a sense of possibility and reignite a visceral energy for life. What are some physical activities to increase the life force?

Shame, guilt, or being overly apologetic or acquiescent can follow negative states of mind. While these emotional states are part of being human, they are not very effective and they also inhibit the possibility of change. These states can often lead to self-deprecating behavior. The horse will often respond to these emotions with aggression and may mirror the stylistic way in which the person is self-negating. For example, the horse may threaten to kick or bite the person, which makes me wonder if the person metaphorically kicks or bites at herself.

Common schemas in these states of mind include:

- Consumed by the way things *should be.*
- Overwhelming need to control.
- Unable to deal with ambiguity.
- Unable to deal with lack of structure or order.
- Fixed in rigid standards of *acceptable* behavior.
- Extreme concepts of right and wrong.
- Overwhelmed with fear of inadequacy.
- Unable to ask for or accept help from others.
- Overly concerned with the expectations of others.
- Fear that nobody respects me or sees my virtues.
- Others are to blame for discomfort and lack of confidence.
- Not looking for solutions or possibilities.
- Lack of self-worth.
- Fear of being defective or that "something is wrong with me."
- Withdrawal or arrogance as a cover-up for feeling inadequate.
- Worry about what others think to the point of paralysis.
- Unable to entertain new perspectives.
- Panic results in working harder and faster.
- Life seems unfair.
- Judgmental toward others.
- The *cup is half empty* or worse yet, it's empty.
- Always looking at what's wrong or not working.

Positive shifts in perspective can include:

- There is so much to learn.

- By being open to learning, I create the future I want.

- It is okay not to know everything.

- I do not need to be perfect.

- I can focus on my gifts and attributes.

- I have something to contribute to others.

- I am responsible for how my life is turning out.

- I acknowledge that some things are possible and some are not. I am at peace with what is.

- What I do is meaningful. My future has many possibilities and I am committed to fulfilling them.

- Life is a gift and I am grateful for being alive.

- I am not worried about "what others think."

- The *cup is half full* or better yet, it's full.

EGE provides a powerful opportunity to identify moods and attitudes that are inhibiting the change process. Horses that are present during the therapy and/or coaching process reflect the person's underlying attitude, independent of what the person is saying with words. Identifying these attitudes allows clients to re-examine how past events shaped the stories they have hidden under the surface or buried in their soma. The combination of re-interpreting limiting beliefs and attitudes, shifting somatic constrictions in the body, and allowing the horse to be the mirror of these aspects dramatically increases a person's ability to develop resilience, a positive self-identity, confidence, and new paradigms for living a satisfying life.

The horse as the guide is a powerful and unique component of the change process because participants know that the horse is indeed impartial and thus can trust the horse's reflection of their underlying moods and fears about change with less self-judgment.

The horse mirrors people's underlying feelings or moods about the conversation or subject matter they are examining, whether it is discussing past events or imagining future outcomes. The facilitator navigates between what is old and what is new, helping the individual interpret the horse's response and how it relates to the person's current contemplation.

During the EGE process, the participants' judgments and interpretations are evaluated while maintaining focus on new stories about the future and looking to distinguish between automatic reactions versus choosing new outcomes. By developing self-awareness of somatic responses coupled with interpretation of those responses, the participant develops choice in how to respond under pressure and conflict.

In earlier chapters it was discussed how one of the objectives in the early phases of the change process is to identify the beliefs, judgments, and fears that are inhibiting the change process. Once an awareness of these inhibitors is achieved, the facilitator can assist the client in noticing when open curiosity has disappeared and re-direct the inquiry towards further exploration

SUMMARY

Fear, negative attitudes, and judgments do the following:

- Stop learning.

- Prevent change in thought, behavior, and action.

- Trigger negative self-concepts and judgment of self and others.

- Create a constriction of one's core life force.

- Limit self-awareness and self-exploration.

- Prevent authentic responses to current situations.

- Cause reactive responses versus choosing how one wants to respond.

- Can become the predominant somatic organization, leading to dis-ease.

- Reflect the memories of historical experiences.

- Inhibit imagination and creativity.

Somatic conditioning and energetic contractions of the body:

- The natural energy flow of the body moves vertically, up and down.

- Contraction of the life force occurs horizontally.

- Constriction of energy can be a low-grade, chronic state of contraction or intense rigidity.

- Conditioning and contraction can be associated with traumatic, historic incidents.

- Contraction along any one of the horizontal bands can affect the whole nervous and/or organ system.

- Our state of contraction influences how we perceive our external world and ourselves and ultimately limits our sense of possibilities.

- As one releases contraction there is a disorganization, a discomfort, a new feeling.

- As one relaxes and opens, one needs to reduce the tendency to seek homeostasis and revert back to the pre-existing (familiar) contraction.

Moods and attitudes

- Mood is a physical presentation of a person's judgments, assessments, and opinions.

- Moods can be learned habits and interpretations that become automatic.

132

- Moods and attitudes create a sense of possibility or no-possibility.

- Moods and attitudes directly affect a person's capacity to take action and coordinate effectively.

- Moods and attitudes directly affect the quality of a person's relationships with others.

EGE is Somatic and Intuitive

THE IMPORTANCE OF SOMATICS

Somatics – the art and science of the inter-relational process between awareness, biological function, and environment, all three factors being understood as a synergistic whole: the mind, body, spirit as a unity; the unity of the self.

Soma – "the experience of the body" as subjectively experienced by the consciousness that inhabits it.

The word *somatics* comes from the Greek word *soma*, which translates as "the living body in its wholeness: the mind, the body, and the spirit as a unity." Somatics as a facilitation tool incorporates the validity of historical conditioned responses to earlier experiences, the mental ability to re-interpret, and the value of recurrent practice to create change in thought and action.

Some interpretations of somatics include the focus on the way the soma itself responds to the environment; other interpretations focus on the way the mind interprets the soma, or one's physical response.

Equine Guided Education, when done well, focuses on the interconnectedness of the soma to the environment: the unity of the mind/body/spirit, as our "animal body," in the living environment (wherein the lack of unity with the living surroundings causes dis-ease).

Horses, wild animals, and nature can teach us that our mental processes get in the way, literally clouding our ability to accurately interpret our experiences. We are conditioned by our educational systems to over-emphasize our logical process and its need to interpret, quantify, and qualify our experience (whether consciously or unconsciously), neglecting the underlying biological instincts that we are responding to before thought. We learn not to trust our feelings, but rather to trust what we think we *should or shouldn't do*. We are often trained in our social communities to judge feelings as wrong or invalid.

The ability to shift behavior and how we think cannot develop solely by creating new ideas or goals. Our historical experiences (our body memories) and subsequent mental interpretations create our habits and patterns of behavior. As we grow into different levels of maturity, habits and patterns that worked well earlier in life may now produce limitations or interference. We eventually figure out that simply changing our mind or attempting to change our behavior is not as easy as it would seem. To make sustainable shifts in our behavior and ways of thinking, we have to "embody" these new schemas. The path to achieving such embodiment is established through a series of recurrent physical practices integrated with new interpretations about the meaning of our life and the impact of our actions or inactions. This is where the latter phases of the change cycle begin and the EGE process often includes more active exercises.

During EGE sessions, somatic distinctions include the body language, mood, and non-verbal energetic qualities of the horse, the client, and the facilitator. A good EGE facilitator knows that the body responds to the environment first. It tells the story of how we relate to our environment, to others, and to a particular situation in the moment.

It is one skill to be able to read the body language of the horse, but an entirely different skill to read the person's body language and somatic presentation and how it is influencing the session. EGE facilitators require the additional skill of staying present, open, and non-judgmental during the session from a *somatic perspective*. The horse in the EGE process is not only reading the client's somatics, it is reading the facilitator's somatics too. The horse that senses when the facilitator is ungrounded or off center may begin reflecting the facilitator's underlying moods and attitudes rather than the client's. As mentioned earlier, this requires that the facilitator understand her potential influence and her somatic presentation and that she continually practice her own somatic presence.

The following is an excerpt from the chapter on "Somatics and Spirit" from the book, *Horse Sense for the Leader Within*.

136

The raven, sitting atop my prayer tree, talks to me. The horses in the field whisper words of wisdom. The wind nurtures my face with her gentle touch one day and the next whirls dust into my eyes so I cannot see. The earth holds me up when I am sad and wish to be invisible. She is always there for me, always waiting to catch my fall or enjoy my success. Sometimes she asks me to look at her beautiful spring poppies dancing in the wind. She tells me through the hawk's call that I already know the answer to my own question. I listen. I remember that I belong. Her sand feels soft and warm as I walk upon her. The taste of her berries makes me smile. It's hard to feel sad and lonely when I am with her.

The wounded child, who cuts herself so she can feel her pain (labeled in a mental institution with words I do not understand), sits on the ground as the black-and-white mare stands over her. The horse mother nurtures the girl. She has not been asked to care. She just knows that this child needs her love and patience. The human mother knows this too, so she drives the girl the long hour and half to the ranch. She knows that no human can save her daughter, but a horse can.

The mother sits outside, waiting, healing herself in the sun and the cool afternoon breeze without knowing. The girl tells the mare about getting behind in school, her friends doing drugs and pushing sex, her mother's disappointment with her. She loves her mother but she is not who her mother wants her to be. She does not want to disappoint her mother, but she has to be true to her own inner calling, one her mother doesn't understand.

She touches the horse's soft coat, and breathes the same breath. The breeze tickles her face. Her heart opens. She talks about the girl she draws on paper, over and over again, with dark lines under her eyes and tears running down her face. Her mother says that her drawings are morbid. But the horse thinks otherwise. And so a healing begins. The girl learns to be herself and to set appropriate boundaries with her mother. Rather than cutting herself, she tells her mother that her comments are hurtful. And the mother learns to listen to her child, to see her with new eyes. This child of hers is an artist, one who walks lightly on the earth. She will not be an accountant, she will not live a "practical" life; it is not her destiny to do so. And so the mother, without knowing it, awakens to the wisdom of the earth. She no longer sees her daughter through human eyes. She finally recognizes and embraces her daughter's spirit. They drive the long road back to the city holding hands.

The somatics of the girl and the mother resonate with the somatics of the environment. Each is healed by the other. Where one begins and the other ends is inexplicable. The mysterious and magical healing of the horse and the girl, the mother and the sun, cannot be defined in textbooks or recorded on tape. And yet, witnessing such beauty brings tears to one's eyes and warms a tired heart.

Somatics involves the pulsing, connected nature of all things, the sensate wisdom within all living beings: mind, body spirit in its wholeness. Perhaps the human's first angst begins with disconnecting from the great mother, the ultimate nurturer of the spirit. The notion that we can heal our hearts and find ourselves by just getting outside and listening, feeling, touching, smelling, tasting, is too easy. It doesn't require an education. It's scary to think that the years we have spent training our minds might be somewhat insignificant. It's just too easy to go outside and let nature do the healing.

Nature is not scientific; she needs no explanation, logical reasoning, or justification. She wasn't trained to justify her actions, to quantify her results. She is ever-present, all accepting, non-judgmental, patient, and resilient. At the same time she is simultaneously merciless, sometimes feeling cruel in her non-sentimental swipes. She is forever practical and wise. She is the pure embodiment of somatic sensibility.

In diagram 4, the concepts of somatics as separated into the three elements of mind, body spirit, don't live in the fixed form of the circles they are associated with. Each concept is dynamic. For example, the world and its association with a person's spirit can go at the center instead of the outer circle. Or the mind and its concern of others could be in the outer circle or in the middle circle. Each part of our somatic experience doesn't live in circles. When a person is out of balance, one aspect may be overly emphasized or under emphasized. Make sense? Remember to allow your own curiosity to be present as you explore the different relationships between self—other—world and mind—body—spirit.

Diagram 4: Understanding the relationship between self—other—world and mind—body—spirit

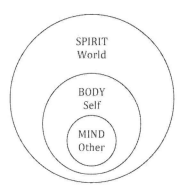

Some professions focus on the way the soma itself responds to the environment; others focus on the way the mind interprets the soma's response. What I am particularly interested in is the interconnectedness of the soma and the environment: the unity of the mind/body/spirit and the living environment (wherein the lack of unity with the living surroundings causes dis-ease). I believe that this is where spirit lives: the simple but bold truth that we (as a mind/body/spirit) are a part of the whole.

The more we quest for the answer to *who am I*, the more we begin to realize that it isn't about "I" at all, but rather, who I am in relation to *how I* contribute to the greater whole. When we recognize that the core self of every individual is inextricably entwined with the natural environment, self-development directs its focus on *how am I destined to contribute or relate to the whole to which I am fundamentally connected.* By seeing the self as part of the whole, we transpose the symbolism of body/mind/spirit to self/other/world.

The Body

The body is the physical aspect; our animal body (labeled as the SELF in the diagram) as it relates to, contributes to, or takes away from the environment. The body holds all of the experiences and memories of our lives. It relates to the environment first. It is the part of the self that we need to listen to most – the first informant – the first interaction with change. In order to change our environment, we first have to change ourselves, change the way our body interfaces with and responds to the environment. I like the saying by Barbara Rector, "I take full responsibility for myself and in so doing contribute to the safety of the group." This implies that we cannot change others, but can only change ourselves, and by changing ourselves, we contribute to the potential change of our greater environment.

The Mind

The mind is in the social domain of *other*. How we think about and relate to others, how others relate to us, is the next immediate interface we have with the whole of the environment. We are social animals; our instinct is to care about how others perceive us. Often it is either our perception of how others see us, or how others tell us they perceive us that can produce either a healthy or an unhealthy self-perspective. For example, the story of the girl and her mother illustrates that the original dis-function arose out of mental interpretations by both the mother and daughter, and traveled outward to the daughter's interpretation of others, including friends, teachers, etc.

Some ancient theories pose that to achieve mindfulness requires detachment from the mind itself. Interestingly enough, the art and science of astrology sees the *intellect* as only one of ten basic components of the human psyche. My favorite astrologer, Jessica Murray, writes:

> *Humanistic astrologers see the mind as a tool of the life purpose, which itself is a tool of the soul. Far from being the seat of consciousness, the mind is merely an apparatus, a marvelous piece of*

140

equipment that serves or doesn't serve the whole person. There is quite a gap between this view and the way most of us operate . . . It is a very old idea that in order to achieve excellence in any endeavor, from art and war to athletics, the mind must be disciplined into a concentrated state. The more practical of these traditions do not mention the lofty goal of enlightenment, but every one of them – from ancient martial-arts exercises to Silva Mind Control – proposes that our incessant internal yak-yak-yakking is an encumbrance to clarity and effectiveness.

The Spirit

The spirit correlates with how the self orients with respect to the world, how the self connects to the environment and the larger cosmos of reality. This includes an individual's beliefs, ethics, and values. It includes the underlying destiny or life purpose of the individual. The mystery of past life experiences and the innate desire to contribute to the whole live here. This seems to be the least studied area of somatics, perhaps because it is the most indefinable, the most mercurial and mysterious of the somatic domains. Historically reserved for witches, shamans, and quacks, this domain of somatics is the missing piece to current studies of dis-ease and what causes dis-ease. By re-connecting to her spiritual longing, this girl was able to re-interpret herself in relation to others in her life.

In many indigenous cultures, the shaman or medicine person's primary function is not actually to heal the individual, but to heal the dis-harmony between the community of people and the natural environment within which the people live. I like the shift from disease (a focus on what is wrong with the individual's physical body or mind) to dis-ease, meaning more directly that the individual is not in ease or flow with the surrounding environment, which is made up not only of family, friends and the human community, but also the rocks, trees, wind, birds, and animals (or lack thereof) that surround the individual. Transferring the focus from what is wrong with the individual (loaded with human judgments) to re-connecting to the original self (the spirit of the person) and the local environment allows an important shift in the individual's ability to develop a healthy self-image and more effective habits of relating to others and to the whole.

To access the spirit requires imagination and curiosity, a form of *not knowing and not requiring an answer*. The native imagination begins in the realm of feeling and sensory awareness and emerges into consciousness through an ability to suspend certainty. It is in this precise way that horses can become our teachers, offering us a whole new world of sensory awareness where new insight and new interpretations can develop.

Being in the presence of horses requires that we develop our other senses because the only way we can develop communication and partnership with them is through being present to somatic experience and listening to our intuitive sensations. When we are in our heads, judging ourselves or doubting our intuition and somatic senses, we are literally not safe for the horse to relate to. When our mind, body, and spirit are aligned (the energy flowing freely within and between), the horse becomes interested and willing to connect.

In team building and leadership development, the reliance on nonverbal communicators as the significant tools for developing relationships forces us into *practicing* leadership principles rather than *thinking about them*. In this way, we train our willingness to let go of what *we know* for what we *don't know* and this becomes the ground from which we learn and develop new skill. In this more authentic state we develop a natural presence for leadership as opposed to a positional authority of control.

Aristotle spoke of "ethos" as a type of leadership in which a leader influences others to change their values and thus their performance. He explained that ethos is not what a person says or promises, but it is that person's *way of being* in the world, his or her presence and comportment, that inspires others to follow and be open to his or her ideas. A leader's success depends on her ability to lead a group of people creatively, effectively, and with exquisite vision through a variety of challenges and breakdowns. To do this well, a leader needs to be able to listen with an open mind, communicate goals without emotional baggage, and assist each team member in finding a sense of purpose about their work.

Effective leaders understand that this type of leadership is a skill that is trained and developed, refined and nurtured. Michael Jordan, the famous basketball player, said it well when describing his coach in his book, *For the Love of the Game:*

> *As a player you connected with the atmosphere the coach created. With Phil Jackson it was like we were in harmony with each other in the heat of the battle. We were comfortable not only with each other but also with the situation no matter how difficult the moment. We were able to find peace amid the noise, and that allowed us to figure out our options, divine solutions, and be clear-headed enough to execute them. That's what Phil brought to the Chicago Bulls and that's what we all connected with. That's one of the reasons we became so successful for so long. That presence, that peace of mind, that connection between the team and the coach was more valuable than anyone possibly could know. But that was Phil. That was who he was at the core of his being. It wasn't contrived. He taught us to find peace within ourselves and to accept the challenges; whatever they may be at whatever moment they appear. It wasn't just an intellectual passing out information. We were able to see the embodiment of those thoughts every day.*

SOMATICS AND SPIRIT

The body is the primary information gatherer, whether you are a human, dog, horse, or bird. The body responds to the environment first; the mind comes along after the fact and interprets the energetic stimuli present. At a biological level, the body responds with immediate speed, before thought, determining safety vs. danger.

Each person is a soma contributing to the energetic aliveness of the environment. Each animal and plant is also a contributing soma. Even the wind, the sun, the mist, the rain are contributing somas. And so begins the realization that each is influencing the other all the time, before thought, before cognition, before rationality. What can be gained by feeling the soma at its beginning, at its first and continuing interface with the environment? A stick can become a fairy wand or a weapon to defend the self. A shell can become a treasure, giving us strength and power.

Animals and nature teach us that our mental processes get in the way, literally clouding our ability to feel ourselves. We are the judgmental animals. Often it is our interpretations (self-directed or felt from others) that begin to disconnect us from the world at large. We learn not to trust our feelings. Instead, we judge our feelings as wrong or invalid. When we reconnect to the land and animals, we re-member that our immediate environment, not our mental acuity, provides the answers and affirms our sensate feelings. By becoming part of our environment we have the opportunity to re-learn how to trust our "feelings," our sensate responses. As a result we are better able to answer the primal questions like, "Do I feel safe?" "Am I scared?" "Do I feel connected?" "I am I doing what I am supposed to be doing with my life purpose?"

Nature reminds us, forces us, insists not only that we feel, but that we become aware of how we feel – that we need to trust how we feel. Sometimes the wind is soft and nurturing and other times it is scary. As we awaken to the deeper meaning of the inter-relatedness of all things, we are forced to realize how disconnected we have become. The feelings and sensations that arise from the earth can become overwhelming for some.

Perhaps some of the modern-day angst that many people are experiencing is really the angst of the earth herself. Perhaps the sadness we sometimes feel is really someone else's sadness traveling on the silent threads of the air around us. Perhaps the girl who cuts herself is truly connected to the pain of the whole. The hope is that she continues to re-source herself by being with animals and nature, to give her the emotional, spiritual and physical strength to let her own unique voice and expression grace all those around her.

INTUITION

Logic deals with concepts of money and concern about what others will think about who you are and what you do. Intuition deals with your spiritual longing and your purpose in life. From the book, *Gift of Fear*, by Gavin de Becker,

> *... Trusting intuition is the exact opposite of living in fear. .... Intuition connects us to the natural world and to our nature. Freed from the bonds of judgment, married only to perception, it carries us to predictions we will later marvel at ... Rare is the expert who combines informed opinion with a strong respect for his own intuition and curiosity. Curiosity is, after all, the way we answer when intuition whispers, "There is something there."*

The *Encyclopedia Britannica* defines intuition as the power of obtaining knowledge that cannot be acquired either by inference or observation, by reason or experience. Intuition is an independent source of knowledge that we cannot exactly define or quantify, a precognitive knowing of oneself in relation to the outer world. It is informed by energetic sensations and responses. It arises out of the unknown landscape of our physical being and the energy of the local and non-local environment. If we allow our intuition to enter into our cognitive space uncensored by our historic conditioning, it can inform us in profound ways.

By developing the capacity to listen to our intuition, we can re-connect to our inner sense of well-being and right alignment. We allow our emotional intelligence to inform and assist us. In this authentic state, we create a *spaciousness* in which we sense the world around us, gathering information from all of our senses. We listen to the non-linear insisting of our spirit calling us to pay attention to its message.

In many of the EGE sessions in which I work, clients are trying to solve intuitive problems with logical solutions. They come to me once they have exhausted all attempts to find logical solutions to their situations. A common report is, "I am not sure why I am here, but I feel called to the horses." I believe when I hear that statement that the person's spirit is calling out for help. An intuitive response to address the disharmony from within has emerged. Through the EGE process, many of these people find the courage to face into their dilemmas and make choices to change their trajectories that once seemed impossible.

When we are in an intuitive state of mind, our senses are not clogged with the judge's mental chatter. We are not thinking. We are just being present to our inner calling. When we listen to our intuition, there is effortlessness or grand simplicity. When we don't, we spend days, weeks, or even years punishing ourselves for not paying attention to that below-the-radar feeling that we didn't follow. How can we forgive ourselves and regain our basic animal right to sense the world from an energetic perspective?

It is important to remember that as animals, we live within our own biological and instinctual habits. At one time, we too depended on our intuition and energetic responses to stimuli for our survival and these traits still reside inside us, often rusty and uncared for. Unfortunately, our cultures and social systems often deny these important qualities. A common example is the five-year-old child who asks his mother, "What's the matter, Mommy?" And the mother replies sternly, "Nothing is the matter!"

This response in essence tells the child that what he picked up via his bodily sensations is incorrect. These repeated, untruthful responses to one's inquiries build the story that one's own intuition is incorrect and cannot be relied on. This social negation of our somatic responses to each other follows us into adulthood.

Through our early years, we receive tremendous social pressure to negate these sensations. We are often told that what we are feeling is not true. We tend to rationalize our decisions with external, socially accepted stories that ultimately become convoluted and isolating. As a culture, we do not hold another's intuitive abilities as a virtue and thus do not respect the intuition of others.

In the example of the mother and son, she did not take care of his intuition in her untruthful response to his question. How many times can you recall when friends or loved ones have asked you if you are upset and you shrugged them off? Does this take care of their dignity? Does it take care of yours? We are conditioned to respond to others in such a way as to avoid discomfort or confrontation. Often this leads to dulling of the self and, in extreme cases, suffering. At some point, either the spirit self decides enough is enough – it feels that it is dying from lies and suppression – or the physical body breaks down as the energy it takes to suppress the intuitive calling becomes too much to deal with.

By the time we are young adults we no longer rely on our sensations or intuitive senses to give us feedback about the world. We may not even notice that our body is in a flight-or-fight response. We have lost the skill of speaking from our "feeling self" because we often cannot ground our perceptions in factual words. We do not trust that others will believe us or respect us. The dilemma remains: How do we balance our inner sensations with our outer push into the world?

With horses (and other animals), the only real communication we have with them is our intuition and somatic interpretations. We listen to them, and they to us, via subtle energetic cues. The language of animals is universal. This is why the horse is a worthy teacher for us to relearn how to accommodate and utilize our nonverbal communication skills. In their mysterious way, horses open our intuitive channels of listening and perceiving. How and why they do it is not of much interest to me. What is interesting to me is that it is consistent among all of the clients I work with, regardless of their educational background or socio-economic status.

Thus, horses provide a great opportunity to keep us on track, always reminding us to embody the moment and forcing us to practice being centered and grounded by responding only to authentic engagement in which our mind, body, and spirit are aligned and in unity.

INTUITIVE LISTENING TO SOMATIC SENSATIONS

Communication means in its simplest definition to share one's ideas or to evoke an understanding in another. It is essentially a form of energetic transaction. Communication has texture, form, and a quality or mood associated with it. Think of the image of one horse running towards another horse with its ears pinned back and its head and neck stretched with teeth bared.

You might quickly say, "Wow, that horse is angry." Another person might say, "That must be the lead mare." Multiple interpretations can arise out of a single transaction.

Communication is comprised of verbal and non-verbal cues and body language. Some examples of communication via these somatic signals include body posture, tone of voice, energetic mood, rhythm of the breath, and muscular tone (tension vs. relaxation). In the human sciences, research has shown that only 7% of our human communication is word content. The other 93% is comprised of tone of voice and body language.

As discussed in the chapter "The Horse As Guide," EGE relies on exploring the tone or quality of interactions versus rushing to interpretations and conclusions. Before we interpret what is being communicated, we practice noticing the tone or mood of the interaction. We ask, "What is the quality or tone of the body language I am observing?"

Some examples of non verbal body language include:

Visual stimuli

- Somatic body posture of a person
- Appeasing
- Not open
- Defensive or rigid posture
- Weight on feet
- Tilt of head
- Apologetic
- Acquiescent
- Eyes: soft or hard
- Mouth: tight, pinched, too smiley

- Diaphragm: sunken in, curved
- Breathing: quality of breath
- Shallow
- Short
- Long and resigned

Auditory stimuli
- Tone of voice
- Soft spoken or too loud
- Breath

Sensate-Intuitive; 6th Sense/Animal Sense
- Mood
- Energetic tone
- Quality of breathing and breath moving through body
- Biological instincts and drives
- Being honest vs. withholding
- Less of a story, more of a feeling
- Not about the words they are saying as much as the tone or quality of the energy

Other Sensual perceptions
- Ions in air
- Wind and weather patterns
- Heart rate
- Blood flow
- Density or energy of the air

- Clairvoyance
- Telepathy
- Touch
- Blood memory
- Past life impressions or senses

The Magical and Mysterious Wisdom of the Natural World

During my studies of animal social systems at U.C. Davis in the early 1980s, my native beliefs about the natural world came to the foreground with a deep resonance and practicality. It was then that I first realized that my native view had been all but forgotten by most of the people I met walking down the street. In fact, it was often looked down upon. Spending time alone at the U.C. Davis Raptor Center or in the non-domestic ward at the U.C.D. Veterinary School allowed me new opportunities to explore the intricacy of non-verbal communication between my animal friends. I had found an arena where I could explore my ideas without complete judgment from others. To this day, I am still fascinated with understanding humans through the animalistic lens that *we are our biology, just like any animal.*

We are animals ourselves, driven by the same biological drives as our other animal relations. We feel and sense our surroundings and others with our somatic senses. I like to think of our somatic self as our animal self, our somatic body as our animal body, responding to the environment around us like a fine-tuned dousing rod.

While I had grown up in an environment where I was in nature every day, I began to realize that other people had not. And that as a result, those who did not have a history of rich relation with the natural world were lacking compassion and a sense of connection deep down inside.

In direct correlation to widespread use of machinery, electricity, and technology driven by the industrial age (and now the age of technology), the indigenous knowledge that we are an integral part of our natural world has virtually disappeared among the masses. Some children do not even know that oranges grow on trees. They think they come from Safeway.

We are desensitized every moment we live in our homes, walk on a busy street, ride the subway, or text on our phones.

We are discouraged from listening to our sensations, because it can simply be too much overstimulation to feel the harshness of the energy created by machines and electricity.

THE EPIDEMIC OF DESENSITIZATION

Schools were originally established to dummify our children – dumb them down – strip them of feeling. It's easier to control future citizens this way. Once stripped of our own sensate wisdom, we can be properly conditioned to behave appropriately and to believe what we are told. To learn more about how our schooling system strips us of our senses, take a look at John Gatto's book, *A Different Kind of Teacher*. Also take a look at Al Gore's book, *Assault on Reason*, in which he talks directly about how the U.S. government uses fear as a manipulative tool to keep the masses in control. Following is a brief excerpt from John Gatto's discussions:

> *Schools train individuals to respond as a mass. Boys and girls are drilled into being bored, frightened, envious, emotionally needy, and generally incomplete. A successful mass production economy requires such a clientele. Whereas, small business and small farm economies, like the Amish, require individual competence, thoughtfulness, compassion and universal participation. Our own economy requires a managed mass of leveled, spiritless, anxious, family-less, friendless, godless, and obedient people who believe the difference between Coke and Pepsi is a subject worth arguing about . . .*
>
> *What schools are about in their structural design are dependency, obedience, regulation, and the subordination that an orderly system needs. Schools achieve these goals by endless exercises in subordination . . .. Schools make childhood surreal by the application of Kafka-like rituals: They enforce sensory deprivation on classes of children held in featureless, sometimes windowless rooms: They sort children into rigid categories by the fantastic measures of age-grading and standardized test scores: They train children to drop whatever they are occupied with and to move as a body from room to room at the sound of a bell: They keep children under constant surveillance, depriving them of private time and space: They forbid children their own discoveries,*

*pretending to posses some vital secret which children must surrender
their active learning time to acquire.*

   *Herbert Spencer, the great British philosopher and publicist on
Darwinism, wrote a remarkable book entitled Education in the early
1860s in which he pronounced government schooling a preposterous
endeavor doomed to failure. He said that this would happen because it
deprived children of raw experience and responsibility precisely at the
moment their natural development demanded it. . . . In 1895 the
president of Harvard said this: "Ordinary schooling, by confining
children to books and withdrawing their attention from visual objects,
renders the senses useless. It produces dumbness."*

THE INTERCONNECTEDNESS OF ALL THINGS

We are coming into a time when it is imperative to re-learn
how to listen to and respect our sensate, intuitive animalness.
(Just an interesting note, we don't even have the word *animalness*
in our dictionary.) Yet, getting to know more about our natural
selves requires a humbling, an acknowledgment of our place on
the same plane upon which all animals live and die. We are
part of a larger whole, a web of life, each species linked
intrinsically together in a grand cosmos that scientific reason
cannot quite explain. Nor does it need to. We don't need
science to prove that all is interconnected. This basic instinct
lives inside each one of us.

   When this instinct, this ancient knowing, is broken by
societal pressures and lack of outdoor experience in the natural
world, our animal body becomes wounded. Our spirit self
becomes disconnected, lost from its roots.

   Some of us resort to denying our bodily sensations, relying
on mental acumen alone to get through life. This often works
until our mid-forties or early fifties when the spirit self finally
screams in pain and forces the individual to slow down or stop
by creating actual physical dis-ease. These are often the people
who end up feeling called by horses.

   Many of the professionals who become EGE facilitators
are the more sensate, intuitive types (made wrong for their
sensitivity) who never quite *fit in* or *tooted to their own horn*. Horses
are the messengers – the conduits – back to the natural world.

Because of their archetypal presence, they inspire people from all walks of life, even those that fear them for their size and strength. While hummingbirds and butterflies have similar power and connection to the natural world, horses are unique in their ability to inspire us to change and learn.

As one gains experience and knowledge in the EGE process, it becomes apparent that horses are actually only part of the process of healing humans. Horses guide wounded spirits back to the original mother, the original core of existence – the meaning of life and death. Think for a moment of some of the famous poets – they speak of nature, her calming influence, her spaciousness of mind, her redemption of hope.

Thus it is part of the EGE facilitator's primary function, whether it remains implicit or explicit, to bring people back to the land, to nature, to the animals – and thus to the senses! It is through the process of re-awakening a person's core spirit – the ultimate connection to *the interconnectedness of all things* – that healing is found.

In indigenous cultures, the native shamans or medicine people recognize dis-ease in the individual merely as a symptom of the dis-ease in the whole (also known as the greater cosmos or circle of life), which includes the local surroundings comprised not just of the village people, but the neighboring trees, plants, rocks, birds, and wildlife. In modern times this has far greater reachings, expanding to the non-local web of life on earth.

David Abram in his book the *Spell of the Sensuous* defines the shaman's role in healing and offers insight into the understanding of the *inter-connectedness of all things*:

> *The traditional shaman acts as an intermediary between the human community and the larger ecological field, ensuring that there is proper nourishment, not just from the landscape to the human inhabitants, but from the human community back to the local earth. By her rituals, she ensures that the relation between human society and the larger society of beings is balanced and reciprocal, and that the village never takes more from the living land than it returns to it – not just materially but with prayers and praise. The scale of the harvest or size of the hunt is always negotiated between the tribal community and natural world that it inhabits . . .*

It is only as a result of her continual engagement with the animate powers that dwell beyond the human community that the traditional magician is able to alleviate many of the individual illnesses that arise within the community . . . hence the traditional magician or medicine person functions primarily as the intermediary between human and nonhuman worlds and only secondarily as a healer. Without a continually adjusted awareness of the relative balance or imbalance between the human group and its nonhuman environ, along with the skills necessary to modulate that primary relation, any "healer" is worthless – indeed, not a healer at all. The medicine person's primary allegiance, then, is not to the human community, but to the earthly web of relations in which that community is embedded….The most sophisticated definition of "magic" that now circulates through the American counterculture is "the ability or power to alter one's consciousness at will." In tribal cultures, that which we call Magic takes its meaning from the fact that humans, in an indigenous and oral context, experience their own consciousness as simply one form of awareness among many others. The traditional magician cultivates an ability to shift out of his or her common state of consciousness precisely in order to make contact with the other organic forms of sensitivity and awareness with which human existence is entwined.

Only by temporarily shedding the accepted perceptual logic of her culture can the sorcerer hope to enter into the relation with other species on their own terms; only by altering the common organization of her senses will she be able to enter into a rapport with the multiple nonhuman sensibilities that animate the local landscape. It is this, we might say, that defines a shaman: the ability to readily slip out of the perceptual boundaries that demarcate his or her particular cultural boundaries reinforced by social customs and the common speech or language – in order to make contact with and learn from the other powers in the land.

Magic, then, in its most primordial sense, is the experience of existing in a world made up of multiple intelligences, the intuition that every form one perceives – from the swallow swooping overhead to the grasshopper on a blade of grass, and indeed the blade of grass itself – is an experiencing form and entity with its own sensations and predilections.

This concept is further reinforced by one of the greatest leaders of the twentieth century. Martin Luther King envisioned this in his statement:

> *In a real sense all life is interrelated. All men are caught in an inescapable network of mutuality, tied in a single garment of destiny. Whatever affects one directly affects all indirectly . . . I can never be what I ought to be until you are what you ought to be, and you can never be what you ought to be until I am what I ought to be. This is the interrelated structure of reality.*

Deloria and Wildcat in the book, *Power and Place*, which compares Native American metaphysics and Western science, say:

> *The best description of Indian metaphysics was the realization that the world, and all its possible experiences, constituted a social reality, a fabric of life in which everything had the possibility of intimate knowing relationships because, ultimately, everything was related. This world was a unified world, a far cry from the disjointed sterile and emotionless world painted by Western Science...*
>
> *The Indian world can be said to consist of two basic experiential dimensions that, taken together, provided a sufficient means of making sense of the world. These two concepts are place and power, the latter perhaps better defined as spiritual power or life force. Familiarity with the personality of objects and entities of the natural world enabled Indians to discern immediately where each living being had its proper place and what kinds of experiences that place allowed, encouraged, and suggested . . .*
>
> *Today, as Western science edges ever closer to acknowledging the intangible, spiritual quality of matter and the intelligence of animals, the Indian view appears increasingly more sophisticated.*

LIMITATIONS OF LOGIC AND LANGUAGE

Many philosophers insist that we are separate from animals and the rest of the natural world because we have language. They rationalize that because we can coordinate and plan into the future, we are smarter than animals. Our oral language skills do not prove that we are not animals with biological instincts. These philosophers forget that just because we do not understand how animals communicate and coordinate, doesn't mean they don't.

Elephants have a sophisticated communication system we are only now beginning to understand. When an elephant dies, its herd members come back to the body two years later to scatter the bones. They may go off in different directions, but they plan their return ahead of time. Katy Payne of Cornell University has shown that these dynamic herd animals communicate via infrasonic sound waves and families can split up for weeks and meet again at the same time and place. They can communicate with these sounds that are inaudible to humans up to two and half miles during the day and up to twenty-five miles at night.

Another researcher by the name of Caitlin O'Connell-Rodwell is studying how elephants communicate through the ground, not just the air, using a form of seismic communication. Temple Grandin discusses in her book, *Animals in Translation*:

> *Theoretically we could have extreme perceptions the way animals do if we figured out how to use the sensory processing cells of our brains the way animals do . . . another reason for thinking everyone has the potential for extreme perception is the fact that animals have extreme perception, and people have animal brains. People use their animal brains all day long, but the difference is that people aren't conscious of what's in them.*

Migratory birds, whales, and dolphins also provide examples of sophisticated abilities to navigate into the future. Horses can sense winter weather patterns ahead of time and grow a winter coat to acclimate to this forecast.

Who's to say who is smarter, then? While our rational skills in conjunction with our language skills have created amazing innovations, it is these very innovations that are now threatening not only our ability to survive as a species, but also the earth as a living organism. Are we really so smart after all? Perhaps we are dumber than we think. I guess only time will tell.

157

Regardless of our opinions on intelligence, our attempt to distance ourselves from our animal relations not only detracts from *who* we really are; it sets up a dangerous separation from the natural world. The more separated we become – the more numb to sensation – the more soulless we become. The more soulless we become, the more robotic and lifeless we become. Despair, depression, and resignation have become the predominant moods of our culture. We lose the will to fight for our freedom. We no longer know what freedom really means. We are truly lost. George Carlin sums it up in this statement:

> *The paradox of our time in history is that we have taller buildings but shorter tempers, wider freeways, but narrower viewpoints. We spend more, but have less; we buy more, but enjoy less. We have bigger houses and smaller families, more conveniences, but less time. We have more degrees but less sense, more knowledge but less common sense, more judgment, more medicine but less wellness.*
>
> *We drink too much, smoke too much, spend too recklessly, laugh too little, drive too fast, get too angry, stay up too late, get up too tired, read too little, watch TV too much, and pray too seldom. We have multiplied our possessions, but reduced our values. We talk too much, love too seldom, and hate too often . . .*
>
> *These are the times of fast foods and slow digestion, big men and small character, steep profits and shallow relationships. These are the days of two incomes but more divorce, fancier houses, but broken homes. These are days of quick trips, disposable diapers, throwaway morality, one night stands, overweight bodies, and pills that do everything from cheer, to quiet, to kill. It is a time when there is much in the showroom window and nothing in the stockroom.*

RECONNECTING TO OUR ANIMAL NATURE

When one looks at the vastness of the animal kingdom, it is impossible to assert that we humans are somehow dramatically different than other highly evolved animals except that we live out of balance. The assumption that our form of communication is somehow better or more sophisticated does not make any rational or reasonable sense in the big picture of reality. To acknowledge our place in the animal kingdom allows us the possibility of re-learning how to use our other senses, our *animal senses* waiting patiently to be recognized and encouraged. These sources of natural wisdom can lead us out of hopelessness and into courageous action.

Our psychic, intuitive senses are mysterious and magical. They can connect us to the past and the future. They can travel on silent waves across the world. They have the power to heal, to accept, and even to imagine the healing of ourselves and the whole.

It is in this new reality that horses and other animals become our teachers, encouraging us to develop our sensations, to trust our ancient knowing abilities. They teach us that truly *being in the moment* allows one to live gracefully with the unknown. We do not need scientific justification or research to prove that the power of our imagination and the nonverbal skill of our will can change our trajectory. We do not need to wait for proof that the magic and mystery of the natural world contains all of the information we need to heal our planet and ourselves.

Perhaps horses have been selected by the cosmos and her other creations to be the messengers because we so readily identify with them. They are an undeniable visual reflection of ourselves, the environment, and the living senses in its wholeness. We easily identify with their archetypal virtues of strength, beauty, power, courage, wildness, and dignity. Perhaps we have more compassion, and therefore more willingness to listen to the horse than to a dragonfly or red-legged frog.

If we focus on what we have in common with horses and other animals, we see that many of the factors that influence other vertebrate species also influence our precognitive approach to life. We may be unaware of how our biology dictates our fears, ambitions, choices and decisions. Our biological underpinnings are further concealed by long-standing cultural and psychological beliefs that we can reason our way through life by intellect alone. However, many of us learn by trial and error that we cannot simply change our behavior and actions by making a decision to change. Our body holds all of our history, our memories and experience.

We can tell our mind to think new thoughts, but we also need to connect those thoughts to our body's experience and to our spiritual underpinnings.

The majority of people with whom I work are successful by any cultural standard. They have the right car, a nice house, and a great job title, but they are in a crisis of meaning. They often cannot understand *what is wrong* with their lives. Yet their intuitive selves know that their mind/body/spirits are out of alignment. Their spirit selves have become disconnected from the whole.

In order to create sustainable change in how we respond to the complexities of our lives, we need to understand our biological predisposition to be in relationship to the larger whole. Many of us are so busy with modern technology, career advancement, and the quick consumer fix that we have forgotten our need to be part of the natural world. As our busy lives spiral us away from the natural world, the subconscious wisdom of our biological makeup calls us back. Our increased fascination with animal biology, native cultures, shamanism, and altered states of consciousness provides pathways for us to reconnect to the natural world.

This desire to reconnect explains the dramatic growth in the equine and pet industry over the last several years. We are finding new ways to bring animals into our lives. In the past, many of our relationships with animals were based on how the animal could be used for human benefit, like canaries in mines, horses and sled dogs for transportation, barn cats for rodent control. Now people keep animals because they want to have an intimate relationship with another living being. Dogs, cats, horses, and birds are becoming our children.

In 1999, $20.9 billion was spent on pets (not including horses). Over 60 percent of all American households have at least one dog or cat. The average American household spends more money on pet food than it does on wine, over-the-counter drugs, candy, or television sets. We spend more money on veterinary services than on coffee, books, video rentals, or computer software. My 86-year-old neighbor, who relied on his horses to plow the fields and drive him to town, would *have a cow* if I told him that people are now brushing their horses' teeth and house-training them.

What is this increased need for interspecies connection telling us? Is it confirming that we have become so disconnected from our own natural social systems of tribes and communities that we are reaching for any animal contact? Have we so damaged trust within our own kind that we are resorting to other species for intimacy and contact? Or have we innately realized that our mechanical and intellectual prowess that created the information age is spiraling us away from our instinctive need to be connected to the natural world?

This need to be part of a greater whole beyond our own species is one reason that we are incorporating the wisdom of the horse back into our lives. Horses still know who they are and operate with complete integrity of their inner emotions and spirit. As honest reflectors of our own animal ways, they can teach us how to listen to our inner drives, desires, and fears. They insist that we respond authentically to ourselves and to others.

This statement by Dominique Barbier, from his book *Sketches of the Equestrian Art*, illustrates some of the virtues gained by staying connected to the natural world:

> *Horses teach us how to ask without aggression, how to love without condition, and how to avoid the destructive side of perfection. They teach us to sublimate oneself through sharing, giving and healing. They teach us to cherish every single moment for its novelty and wonder and remain true to the best traditions of the past.*
>
> *Horses are calling people from all over the world and all disciplines to re-awaken, to learn to listen to their animal bodies. In this re-awakening and learning how to use our animal senses we can re-connect to the Mother Earth and all of her creations. We can learn how to find our own freedom and in so doing let others be free as well. We can learn to create sustainable practices for living in which man and animal can live and flourish in a natural balance with the land and sky.*

Information Processing, Behavior Generation, and the Human Brain

By Janet Crawford

Humans process information and experience through multiple brain systems. Unlike most other animals, instead of relying primarily on preprogrammed instincts and habits acquired through stimulus-response learning, we also process information through complex emotional programming acquired early in life and rational/logical filters that have the capacity to override the other processing systems. The vast majority of our information-gathering and decision-making machinery operates at an implicit level: outside our consciousness, but still calling the shots.

Our response to every situation is the result of a complex combination of all the systems, although for many of us, the conscious rational level is the only one we know to acknowledge. This leads to befuddling situations such as making New Year's resolutions we know are to our benefit, but which we immediately abandon for no apparent reason. Our instinctual programming and emotional patterning is the key to what has happened. It has a logic all its own for blocking our success.

Rational processing takes place in the *neocortex*, the seat of language and original thought. The neocortex is comprised of the large grey lobes you see in depictions of the human brain, and has two hemispheres, popularly referred to as the left and right brains. In the foremost area of the neocortex, located directly behind our forehead, lies the prefrontal cortex (PFC), which mediates an impressive list of functions, including attuned communication, emotional balance, response flexibility (i.e., the ability to override instinct and unconscious programming), empathy, fear moderation, intuition, future-based thinking, and morality.

163

It is precisely these functions that differentiate humans from the rest of the animal kingdom. We can consciously resist our impulses. We act by moral codes. We can think into the future and create things that don't exist today, allowing us tremendous power over our natural environments. We are the only animal in whom a great deal of our neural processing is devoted to imagining various future possibilities and creating advance strategies for dealing with them.

Amy Arnsten, head of the Arnsten Lab at Yale University, calls the PFC "the Goldilocks of the brain . . . it likes everything just right." The PFC is exquisitely sensitive and limited in its capacity. Were we to *really* use rationality and volition to determine our every action, we would instantaneously overload our neural circuitry. We rely instead on a combination of instinct and acquired habits to determine the lion's share of our responses.

Instinct exists to automate the patterns that keep us alive, so that the precious resources of the neocortex can be used for more valuable purposes. Human instincts primarily evolved during the millennia spent by our ancestors on the African savannah. Although we've now engineered our way into a society where many of those instincts no longer play a critical role in our survival, they have not been erased from our brain's programming, and they still dictate our behavior.

We can override them, but to do so uses the precious and limited brain resources of the PFC. In addition, resisting instinctual impulses can only occur when we are conscious of the impulse and are motivated to counteract it. For a leader, pitting intellect against instinct is a recipe for ineffectiveness.

A second level of processing occurs in the *limbic system*, which is the seat of emotions and memory. We live in an emotionally illiterate society in which we marginalize emotion as immature compared to our logic circuits. One of the most common requests I hear from the executives I work with is, "Will you help me get emotion out of my organization?" Once they understand how emotions function, however, they realize how undesirable and impossible their request is.

People with damage to the emotional centers of the brain cannot, among many other things, make decisions. They may

164

stand in the cereal aisle for hours deciding between generic and brand name. Emotions provide us lightning-fast shortcuts for processing data. Our brain encodes the outcomes of our life experiences with emotional markers. When similar situations arise, we use those markers to guide the rapid production of a "good" decision. This partially explains why we are predisposed to agree with people we like, even when their logical arguments make less sense than those of someone we don't like.

Each of us acquires unique fundamental emotional patterns early in life, typically before the age of two. The very large mass of the human brain would prove fatal to our mothers were it fully developed at birth. To compensate for this anatomical discrepancy, the human brain grows and matures for many years post partum. In fact, the PFC isn't fully matured until we reach our early twenties, explaining in part the often rash behavior of adolescents. Compared with other animals, we spend an inordinate amount of time dependent upon our parents and community while the brain completes its maturation.

Humans are born with what is referred to as "open neurology." At birth, we cannot self-regulate even such fundamental bodily functions as respiration and heartbeat. Rather, we are dependent on physical contact with the nervous systems of those who care for us to regulate ourselves. In the face of danger or pain, we do not innately know how to interpret the seriousness of those signals.

Our bodies mimic the reaction of those most closely bonded to us in order to learn how to respond to the world. After all, our parents' response patterns enabled them to stay alive long enough to pass their genes along to us. It is at this early stage of development that our most sensitive emotional patterns are encoded. As we mature, our neurology becomes increasingly closed, or self-regulating, but it never closes completely. Those around us continue to have an influence over our bodies and moods.

The downside of these acquired emotional patterns is that they are just one way of filtering the universe, and are not necessarily the best or most functional. They are simply the result of the best conglomeration of the patterns we have been exposed to through our parents and culture. They allow for fast judgment in the moment by creating a top-down set of constraints on how we see the world.

The older we get, the more constrained we tend to become. The insidious nature of our implicit patterns is that they produce judgments that feel like "truth." We tend to see perception as neutral, and assume that, given the same set of inputs, people will "see" the same things. The reality is that our sensory apparatuses are not at all impartial. The same light patterns may strike the retinas of two individuals, but the neural pathways that the brain uses to interpret those light patterns will be very different, based on the prior history of those two people.

Humans are designed to unconsciously assess the emotional state of those with whom they interact. We possess specialized cells called mirror neurons, which track minute details about the physiology of those around us. Our brains compare their physiological state with what it would mean for us, were we to exhibit that behavior. A whole host of variables, including breath rate and depth, skin flushing, muscle tension, microfacial movements, and pupil dilation, are monitored continually outside our conscious awareness.

Our body uses what it detects to assess the emotional state and congruence of those with whom we interact, allowing us to expertly maneuver through social situations by predicting other persons' upcoming behaviors, needs and likes.

A combination of our unique emotional patterns with shared primal codes related to such things as dominance, submission, generosity, and reciprocity governs how we interpret nonverbal signals. Our brain gives far more credence to these assessments than it does to the linguistic content of the messages we receive. Our decision to focus all our attention on someone, to turn away and ignore him or her, or to become argumentative, comes only in very small part from a reasoned thought process. We assess other people before they open their mouths to speak. We think we communicate in words, but the bigger story lies elsewhere.

Deep within the limbic brain lie the *amygdalae,* two almond-shaped structures that, among other functions, detect danger and trigger threat responses. What the brain recognizes as dangerous comprises a complicated mix of preprogrammed "hard-wiring" and references to past experiences.

As humans, we *instinctively* know to be afraid of certain things. We see a stick in the trail and freeze, at least until such time as the brain sorts out that it's just a stick and not a snake. Standing on the edge of a cliff makes us queasy even if our balance is good and we've got a rope to steady us. Fire a gun and the sound makes you flinch. As social animals, we are also preprogrammed to assess status, inclusion, fairness, uncertainty, and difference as vectors of our safety.

Another category of threat comes from our internal library of past negative experiences. Our survival depends on avoiding situations that were unpleasant in the past, so we record very sensitive profiles in our memory banks. Whenever we sense something in the present with enough similarity to a past negative situation, that profile is triggered at lightning speed outside of conscious awareness. In order to legitimize our response, we are likely to generate logical stories about the current situation that may or may not bear any real relation to the actual trigger.

When the amygdalae sense sufficient danger, they redirect control of our actions to the most instinctual level of the brain, the *reptilian system,* which governs autonomic body functions and default reactions, such as fight, flight, and freeze. This redirection phenomenon is called an "amygdala hijack." When we are triggered by strong social cues or negative emotional memories, we can quickly go into fight or flight.

This behavioral mode is easy to spot on the African savannah. In the face of danger, you sprint away as fast as you are able or you strike back physically. In our modern jungles, it shows up in a whole host of less overt ways: withdrawal, avoidance, sarcasm, forgetting one's train of thought at embarrassing moments, making socially inappropriate attacks, etc.

Since we generally believe our actions should be logical and volitional, we usually experience hijacks in one of two ways: We find logical justifications for why we did what we did or we feel inwardly ashamed and perplexed, unable to understand why we "went there."

In summary, we can see that our behavior is governed by a complicated mix of neural inputs. Contributors to the equation are instincts shared by all humans. Another contributor comes from individual emotional patterns that exist largely outside of awareness, combined with the learned responses of a lifetime of experience. The last contributor is rational conscious consideration of the situation, with this last level representing only a small fraction of the brain's processing ability.

Now that we've considered our relationship to instinct and gained some insight about basic neural design, we're ready to explore the connection between science and the extraordinary usefulness of EGE in becoming a skilled leader.

THE POWER OF PRESENCE

One benefit of time spent on the ranch has nothing to do with the horses themselves. Modern life keeps us distracted. Focused on email, traffic, work deadlines, television, and other demands, we spend little to no time in natural environments where we can notice ourselves and the subtle patterns around us.

Our ancestors survived by being keenly aware of their environment. To this day, our biology thrives on presence. Brain scans of long-term meditators show substantially more PFC activity coupled with a lowered propensity toward amygdala activation.

Without slowing down, we also don't give ourselves the chance to reflect on and enjoy what is right about our lives. From an evolutionary standpoint, the ability to successfully detect threat and predict harmful outcomes has more survival value than rosy optimism. Finding what's negative is exactly what the brain, left alone, will do. Because of this negativity bias, we tend to project worrisome scenarios onto the future instead of noticing that the present is usually pretty darned good.

Mark Twain once famously said, "I have suffered through a great many tragedies, most of which never happened." Time spent on the ranch reminds us deeply of the goodness and blessing that surround us.

From that space, with low levels of cortisol (the "stress" neurotransmitter) in our bloodstreams and boosted levels of serotonin (the "happiness" neurotransmitter), our PFC functions well, focus is possible, and we tend to attribute fewer insidious motives to those around us.

AWARENESS OF OUR SOCIAL NATURE

A second area of learning involves reawakening the ability to observe ourselves as part of a social and natural system. Our cultural legacy of individualism, dismissal of emotion and instinct, and belief that man exists separate from nature blinds us to the intricate patterns of interaction at play around us. Without fluency in these patterns, we repeatedly misattribute the causes of both our successes and our deepest frustrations, leaving us with limited power to manifest different outcomes.

During my five days at the ranch, introduction to the horses happened slowly. First, we stood on the outside of the arena, simply observing for quite some time, being present with the horses and looking for patterns in their behavior. Once inside the arena, we quietly mingled with the horses, paying attention to our impulses and feelings.

The horses clearly had different roles of authority. Each had a position and when one horse moved, it influenced the constellation of the entire herd. The horses responded in an entirely different fashion to each human individual in our group. They shied away from some, while approaching others eagerly. The mere presence of a few members of our group seemed to agitate the herd, while others elicited the rare trusting horse behavior of lying down. Without intention, each of us had influenced the system in a unique fashion.

What was it that the horses sensed and to what were they responding? Knowing now that people also possess strong unconscious social instincts, might we be similarly influencing our every human interaction without our knowledge? People leave, become playful, aggressive, disruptive, and inattentive. In short, they do all the things that horses do when interacting with each other. Due to the very limited capacity of the PFC, there's only so much of that reaction we can control, even when we're aware of what's at play and want to regulate our response.

I was immediately struck by how little attention we pay in our daily lives to the patterns of the humans closest to us, even those most vital to our well-being at work and home. We're in far too much hurry to get the task done or be entertained. Such observation doesn't seem necessary in a culture that believes in reliance on logic and will power.

Being with the horses reintroduces us to our membership in the animal world, our fundamental social nature, and the interconnectedness of our natural environment. It asks us to behave in a fashion atypical for modern Westerners, allowing us to witness the influence of our being and putting us in touch with the power of our instinctual, emotional and unconscious biology. From that place, we can start to learn how to leverage instinct and the power of emotion to elicit the responses we desire from those around us.

BEYOND RATIONAL EXPLANATIONS AND SELF-JUSTIFICATION

In the realm of leadership, the most profound level at which EGE works is fostering ownership of the influence of one's "being-ness." Many leaders think the world should react to their intentions, positional authority, and logic. When this doesn't work, blame is placed squarely on the recipient of the communication:

"I give clear direction and *they* don't follow."

"I mentor. I give kudos. Still *they* aren't performing to par."

"I came up with great strategy for the team and I communicated it clearly. My meetings are organized, and my tactical plan is tightly designed. Despite it all, the team lets petty arguments and resentments impede our progress. What's wrong with *them*?"

What's missing is the possibility that something about the leader him- or herself could possibly be the impediment. Instead, their followers should "get over" their emotions or sensitivity. What we now understand is that the brain is designed to respond to social cues and that only a very small portion of our behavior is generated through conscious volition. The leader's every move activates instinctual responses in those around him. Pitting logic against instinct is a losing strategy.

What muddies the water for humans is that we are not solely creatures of instinct. We all possess the ability to construct logical arguments, to override instinct, and to make up stories to explain the world around us. In all our interactions, a combination of conscious and unconscious, volition and instinct, is at play. When we respond instinctually, we seldom recognize it as such. Because of that, it is often hard even for highly aware leaders to discern how much is "me" vs. how much is "them."

The horse brain is much smaller as a percentage of body mass than the human brain. More importantly, the equine neocortex is relatively undeveloped. Horses don't rationalize things, nor do they ruminate on the past or spend time worrying about the future. They don't sense one thing and then reinterpret it through thought. Information is processed instinctually and emotionally. Likewise, the horse is impervious to your verbally expressed intent and stories. The information that determines its response comes from your way of being: how you hold your body and move, the tonality of your voice, the smell of your sweat. Horses are simultaneously more instinctually perceptive and have less to cloud that perception.

In human interaction, we make up stories to explain the situations in which we find ourselves. Individuals rarely accurately assess why they can't find a mate that treats them well, their employees leave for other managers, or people fail to share vital information with them. As an executive coach, I conduct assessment interviews with several coworkers of each client at the outset of the contract. Invariably, my clients are surprised by multiple aspects of how others perceive their interactions. Bottom line: What we think is influencing others is often not what is actually at play.

Nature isn't random. When a horse allows one person to lead it and not the next, it's because of how that person is being or failing to be. Horses don't play intellectual games or hold grudges, nor do they second guess themselves or make up elaborate stories to justify the behavior of the beings in their lives. Horses directly perceive who we are in the present moment and respond accordingly. We may be able to rationalize away our ineffectiveness in interaction with other humans, but horses force us to own the effect we have on others. In this context, individuals who act from intellect and dismiss the power of presence come face to face with their limitations.

One of the most important "energies" social animals assess is congruence. Our biological design ensures that non-verbal behaviors and internal emotional states match. It's impossible to convincingly deliver the line "I'm happy" with sad eyes, a morose tone and hunched shoulders. In fact, recent neuroscience research on the congruence of emotions suggests that people easily assess the emotional state of an object in an animated video, simply by observing its movement, shape, and color. What we think and how our body moves has a natural alignment, and incongruence has physical markers. If we are in touch with our instinct, we allow the dis-ease the incongruence produces to surface as information. But even if we ignore it consciously, it still influences how we respond. Because horses lack the cortical ability to explain away incongruence, the response we get from a horse is pure unadulterated reaction to our presence *in the moment.*

As my week on the ranch wore on, I became more and more present with my thoughts, feelings, and impulses. Slowly, a repeating pattern crept into my conscious attention. I would have a bodily sense of a situation followed quickly by an internal explanation or dismissal. This showed up in my initial experience of one participant: I noticed myself thinking that based on our common interests, I should want to talk to her on break. Despite that, I couldn't muster the interest to have a conversation. I quickly went into stories of judgment and self-esteem: "She's a nice person," "I *should* pay attention to her; she's doing some really cool things," "I'm a bad person for not

172

wanting to talk to her." Still, the feeling of lack of interest persisted. At some point, the story even shifted to "We haven't talked because she's not interested in me and probably doesn't like me!"

All that shifted for me when she approached the horses and they responded by walking away. Just moments before, they'd been frolicking with someone else. *They* didn't have any of my stories or content-based reasons telling them to pay attention or not. All they had to work with was her energetic presence. "Do I need to pay attention?" "Does she have presence?" "Can I trust her as part of the herd?" If not, better to leave her to her own devices. Humans can have a felt sense and override it. Horses can't.

I marveled at how much information I had lost by ignoring my initial sense of the situation and covering it with unnecessary stories. Had I stopped with, "I don't feel like talking with her," and then remained curious and open about where that was coming from, it would have served both of us. As it was, I had spent time shaming myself for not including her, chiding myself for not being an effective networker, and feeling anxious about whether I was liked. The exchanges I did have had a forced quality. After all, with those stories going through my head, her instinctual body had to be detecting incongruence as well. Those early conversations lacked an authenticity that might have emerged had I allowed my instinctual reaction into consciousness with compassion and curiosity.

Over the week, as she became more open and I became more settled and authentic, my felt desire to interact and my ease at approaching her increased. Based on their willingness to play with her, the horses felt the same way.

I'VE BEEN A LOT CLEARER SINCE SUNNY BIT ME

Each student in the program, it seemed, experienced at least one breakthrough moment in which old patterns or new awareness became suddenly illuminated. My magic moment happened on the third day. We were gathered in the center of the arena debriefing the morning, with the horses milling about on the periphery of our circle. Suddenly I felt the strong sensation that a horse was approaching me from outside my visual field. I turned around to see Sunny, a powerful gelding, walking directly toward me with a purposeful gait.

My immediate gut reaction said, "I don't like his attitude, and I'm going to let him know it's not okay." Then my cortical stories kicked into high gear: "For heaven sakes, he's just walking in my general direction. Why do you make everything about yourself?" "If you aren't nice to him, everyone will think that you're an animal hater or paranoid." "I'll take my cue about what to do from the guy next to me. After all, he knows what he's doing."

By that time, Sunny had made it across the arena and had stopped directly between me and my classmate, who I'd secretly named Mr. Horse Whisperer based on his uncanny ability to connect with the equine species. He put his hand on Sunny's shoulder, so I dutifully copied. The moment *my* hand made contact, Sunny spun around and bit my forearm with surgical precision. It was a cold morning and I had three heavy layers on. Despite that, he managed to pull a bit of flesh off my arm. Instantaneously, my neocortex went quiet and I spun into instinctual action. I stomped toward him with the energy of a grizzly bear, my open palm hand shoved toward his face. He reared, spun around, and galloped off.

Upon returning to my friend's farm, where I was staying for the duration of the program, I pondered the connection between the day's events and the patterns in my life. The feeling of the interaction with Sunny, along with the stories that accompanied it, was intimately familiar. My life was full of "Sunnys," people whose motives I didn't trust, but with whom I had told myself I needed to play nice or risk looking inappropriate. That night, I quickly dispatched with several emails asking for information, support, and business that simply didn't feel clean. I had procrastinated for many days and invested considerable psychic energy worrying about how to politely decline without closing any doors or offending anyone. Something big had shifted.

SUMMARY

In order to act with power and intentionality in the world, it is imperative to master one's own biological presence such that the human animals we interact with respond from the best possible instinctual place. It is crucial that we learn how to avoid triggering negative instinctual reactions, and come to terms with the "unfair" and unvarnished truth: Our thoughts account for a very small portion of the message we send to others. Having good ideas and surface-level intentions will not make others follow you. Engaged relaxation, assurance, focus, congruence, and presence will.

I am not advocating that we become pure creatures of instinct, or that "listening to your gut" will always give you the best answer. But intellect is a powerful, yet limited force. Rather than relying on intellect as a one-size-fits-all answer to leadership, we can reconnect with the enduring instinctual logic of our biology, leveraging its wisdom when it leads us in the right direction and skillfully overriding it when it doesn't.

A week spent in relationship with horses puts us back in touch with the degree to which we are part of a natural system, participating in a social "herd" and responding more through instinct than rationality. It's been a while since that day, and I'm still a lot clearer since Sunny bit me.

PREPARING FOR

THE EGE PROCESS

Active Versus Passive Exercises

Knowing whether you are in an active or passive activity with a horse is very important to both horsemanship and the EGE process. Being in a passive relationship with the horse is when you are just *being with* the horse. You are not asking anything specific of the horse in this moment. You are not riding or walking the horse; the horse is free to come and go. Grooming can be either a passive or active activity. When you are in a passive grooming activity, you are just grooming and sharing time. You are not actively asking the horse to pay attention or behave a certain way. You may be letting the problems of the day fall away, feeling yourself and feeling the horse.

When you are focusing on how the horse is standing quietly or teaching the horse some protocols for grooming, you are actively training the horse and are thus in an active activity.

You can ask yourself when you're grooming your horse, "What's my purpose or intention right now? Am I choosing to be in passive or active relationship with the horse?" Grooming the horse before you ride might have a different quality to it than after you ride.

I tend to be in passive relationship when I'm grooming my horses, unless I am particularly focused on teaching young or problematic horse boundaries during grooming time. I'm feeling the horse's mood and attention. I'm being with the horse with no plan or an agenda.

When you are in an active relationship with the horse, you're asking the horse to do something specific, and in order to accomplish this the horse needs to follow your lead. You have a specific goal or training objective. Your objective in horsemanship terms may be to train a new skill in the horse's performance. Or, you could be focused on training yourself as a rider or leader of the horse.

In EGE active exercises, the facilitator is not focused on the client learning how to handle the horse per se, but rather on the client developing a grounded presence, confidence, and focus. The elements that are required to be in a mutually reciprocal relationship with the horse are the same elements required to be in reciprocal relationship with humans. The horse becomes the feedback loop for whether the person is relating effectively or ineffectively.

Active exercises include leading the horse in hand, riding the horse, lunging the horse, and trailering the horse. Leading the horse in hand is never a passive activity because we're asking the horse to partner (to respect our authority and decisions) in a very specific kind of way.

Round pen activities can be either passive or active activities. When you're in a round pen with a horse and being in passive relationship, you're not asking anything of the horse. The horse has the freedom to do what it wants. He can walk towards you or away from you, feign lack of interest, eat grass, whatever.

If you're asking the horse to move around the round pen at a walk or any other gait and you have an intention that the horse needs to perform a specific task, then you are in an active activity. When you are in active relationship you need to establish your authority as the direction setter or leader. You and the horse engage in a team effort to accomplish a goal together, allowing the nuances of relationship to be examined and refined.

A different mindset and self-reflection process is needed for passive versus active activities. It is important for the facilitator, the client, and the horse to know when you're switching from passive to active, because it helps clarify roles and relationships and the subsequent conversations that become available. It also helps the horse to know what is being expected of him in each activity.

Once we are in an active relationship there are all kinds of standards we have about how the horse and human coordinate together. This is where the larger dance comes into play between traditional horsemanship and EGE. For those of you that are still fairly new to this work, take the opportunity to spend time in the more passive relationship activities, and ask yourself, "What's really happening here? What images or stories are coming to me? How is the horse being now? Why is my horse quiet today or not? What's shifting in me or the horse and why?"

When we move into a passive relationship we can change our state of awareness from being focused on a particular activity to becoming curious about what is happening on an energetic level. For example, we can go to the barn and sit quietly, observing the energy of the local surroundings and how the horses are responding. Examine how many horses are relaxed and how many are tense. How are they coping? Each horse has a different coping strategy, just as people do.

Some horses will just dull out emotionally. Other horses will become aggressive or fidgety or try to make contact with something. With some of the passive exercises, what you're doing is grounding yourself in the environment. You're opening your senses to how the energy in the environment shifts and how the horse responds to those shifts.

AN EXAMPLE OF A PASSIVE ACTIVITY

I am in the arena with a few horses at liberty. I don't have a particular goal or plan. I am just hanging out with the horses in the arena. The horses have plenty of room to come and go, to relate or wander. As a horse person, I have to bypass or let go of my horsemanship habits of relating and working with horses. I resist the temptation to relate in my habitual way. Instead, I simply watch the horses. I notice that one horse comes right up to me. I ask myself:

- What shifted in me that allowed her to come to me?

- How is my energy?

- What is her energy?

- Why does she want to come to me now and not before? What changed in the energy between us and the environment that changed our relationship together in time and space?

Take note that I am simply asking a lot of questions, being curious and refraining from fixating on a particular interpretation. My goal here is to stay open and explore as many interpretions as I can come up with. In order to be able to do this, I must refrain from deciding that one interpreation is better than the other. I keep all the possiblities open and available. I actually do not answer the question.

When the horse wants to connect, when the horse disconnects and leaves, these are the questions to ask. If we see everything as a form of energy, we ask, what changed in the energy of our circumstances that opened or closed the possibilities of our relationships at that moment and what changed in me, in the horse, and in the enviroment that the horse may be responding to?

If you're going to move into an action-oriented activity, what changes in the relationship? You need to have a specific role with the horse and the horse needs to have a role with you. What is your intention or reason to change into this activity? What is your purpose?

I like the passive-active distinction because when you switch from a passive activity to an active activity, it's a whole different ball game. It makes you more responsible for your actions. When you're involved in passive exercises, the horses have the choice to relate or not relate. When you're in active relationship, the horses become more vulnerable to people mistreating them.

Active exercises have a much higher rate of stress and burnout for horses. Sometimes, in extreme situations, you can even lose your horse to the point that it does not want to engage with the public anymore.

I've seen situations in which a person has hit the horse with a lunge whip or rope, quite unexpectedly. While this has been extremely rare, only two instances in my twenty years, it has damaged my horse's trust and willingness to participate. The horse will lunge fine for me, but will never lunge in a clinic anymore. All it takes is one time.

I hardly ever lunge the horses anymore, even though it's one of the most brilliant exercises of all. That's the dilemma we each face in doing this work and having our horses involved.

Even when you are leading in hand, you never know what to expect. Some people are very aggressive with the lead rope, and you see your horse having a very negative reaction to the way the person is using the tools.

In both horsemanship and EGE work, while the human may be the leader or guide of the horse in the physical realm, the horse is the guide or leader of the psycho-spiritual realm. This is where EGE really takes off from the platform of horsemanship. In EGE, we want the horse's reflection, that honest clarity.

During the early phases of the change process, the EGE facilitator focuses more on the intra-relational aspects of the client's process, and thus passive activities are primarily used. By intra-relational I mean looking within the self, i.e., how the self relates to others. Passive activities encourage self-exploration, intuitive listening, and new levels of self-awareness. Active activities are inter-relational in that they are focused more on how a person coordinates with others. This includes how the person works toward his or her goals at the same time considering and exploring how others are also relating to the person's presence

Diagram 5: Active and Passive Activities

PASSIVE-Intra-relational	ACTIVE-Inter-relational
Inquiry	Taking action
Exploration and reflection	Leadership
Identifying old stories	Developing confidence
Discovering new stories	Staying focused on a goal
Formulating new direction and purpose	Relationship dynamics
Intuitive	Practical
Self-awareness	Relational awareness
Somatic presence	Somatic dynamics with and between other beings

During the latter phases of the change process, clients begin to do more active exercises with horses because they are practicing taking action – moving forward in their lives. The

EGE facilitator encourages the client to become the direction setter and to take responsibility for the horse's actions and responses. As the direction setter of the horse-human team, the client practices can include topics such as:

- I am responsible for myself and in so doing I contribute to my own safety and the safety of the horse.

- I promise to attend to my inner emotional states.

- I trust that I will be enough to be a good leader for the horse.

- I promise not to over-use my intellect or my rational mind when I work with my horse.

- I promise that I will not judge myself and my horse; we are just learning how to be better partners.

- I will listen to the horse's feedback about my energy and intentions.

- I promise to be the goal setter.

- I promise to be trustworthy.

- I promise to be sincere and authentic.

- I promise to develop my competency to be reliable and consistent.

- I will practice being aware of my mental, physical, and spiritual energy.

- I promise to be a clean slate.

Passive activities

- We are not asking anything of the horse.

- We are just being with the horse.

- We are allowing the horse to do whatever it is doing at any moment.

- We have no desired outcome or goal with the horse.
- We are not being the horse's leader.

Active activities

- Haltering the horse
- Leading the horse in hand
- Moving the horse in round pen
- Lunging the horse
- Riding the horse

Tools for making the transition between active and passive exercises

- Acknowledge that the horse is the guide of the psycho-spiritual realm.
- Notice your own conflicts when your horse is interacting with a participant.
- Remember what your primary goal is with the client.
- Challenge your assumptions about horsemanship.
- Avoid teaching horsemanship, unless you are only teaching horsemanship.
- Pay special attention that the horse is respected in the process, especially during active activities.

Questions to consider

- If my horse starts to nudge or make physical contact with the participant, should I react as a horse person and establish boundaries or shift into EGE?
- How do I manage an exercise so that it does not become about horsemanship, but focuses on the learning objective for the client?

- What if my horse behaves in a way I have never seen before; how do I best respond to take care of the goals of the session, the person(s), and the horse?

- How do I let go of fears that my horse will get ruined by letting other people work with it?

SUMMARY

The primary focus of EGE activities is not on actually completing the activity itself, as is common in traditional horsemanship. It is not about making the horse do something. Rather, it is about what we learn about ourselves in the process of engaging with the horse.

Do not get caught in, "The horse shouldn't be doing that, so fix it, now." What the client is learning is more important than making sure the horse is performing correctly. Let go of the fear that your horse will develop bad habits.

Passive activities are much less likely to create conflict, concern, or dilemma. Active activities require special attention to the concerns of the horse, the client, and the horse owner. Both passive and active activities require the facilitator to step beyond traditional rules of horsemanship.

Choosing Exercises

Choosing exercises depends on a variety of considerations. One primary consideration is what phase of change the participant is in. If the participant is in the early phases of change, passive exercises are best to encourage opening the mind and allowing exploration and imagination to stimulate new thinking and paradigms. If the participant is at the point of change where he or she has developed clear goals and a new course of action, active exercises encourage moving forward, practicing new declarations and embodying the presence required to succeed.

Why do we use the term 'exercises' instead of 'activities'? The term exercise is defined as an activity that is done to practice or test a new skill. It is also considered a process that is carried out for a specific purpose. When we are offering EGE exercises, we are providing a specific process in which the participant is given the opportunity to practice new skills. These new skills can be new ways of thinking, exploring and imagining or they can be new ways of presencing, being present, and embodying their intentions and goals.

Each exercise should have an underlying goal or purpose. This is one reason why knowing what phase of change a participant is in becomes important. For example, in the first phase of change exercises emphasize opening into an inquiry, letting go of judgments and habitual expectations in order to allow time to imagine new scenarios and possibilities.

In the latter phases of change, once a participant has spent time exploring new possibilities and has identified new goals, exercises focus on engaging in specific activities in which they are moving forward and taking new actions towards their goals. These active exercises are also providing practice in embodying the new paradigms.

Practicing team and leadership exercises with horses provides a unique opportunity to work with the whole somatics of the participant. The participant is coordinating mind, body and spirit simultaneously. This is distinct from classroom learning in which only the mind is engaged. It is also distinct from just riding a horse, which is a primarily a physical or bodily practice. EGE practices focus not on becoming a horseperson or training horses in which the primary goal is to get the horse to accomplish a series of actions. EGE specifically focuses on creating a physical presence that is congruent to the intentions (spiritual ambitions) and verbal declarations.

Therefore, I will often remind a participant that the success of the exercise is not to get the horse to perform, even though we may set up the exercise with that intention. The success of the exercise is to gain new insights and new experience. For example, when I offer a leading in hand exercise, I ask the person to declare a goal that is specific to their real life. I then ask them to lead the horse with that intention. I may also ask what the horse represents; as in who do they need to create a relationship with to accomplish their goal?

The horse may represent a co-worker, a boss or a potential client. I emphasize to the participant that the goal of the exercise is not to get the horse from point A to B, but to practice being the leader of their vision. Leading effectively is a combination of confidence, commitment, combined with clear intentions and the energy of moving forward. By leading the horse, we are able to evaluate what in the new declaration has become embodied and where confidence still needs to be developed.

Putting people in an exercise they are not ready for can set up a feeling of failure in the participant and/or the horse. Asking a participant to lead the horse when the participant is no longer clear about who he o she is are or where he or she wants to go is inappropriate. Without clear intention, the horse has no way of sensing the participant's goals and will not move forward. In this situation the participant ends up feeling like a failure. Thus knowing the underlying goals of an exercise and the specific actions to be practiced is very important.

HOW MANY EXERCISES DO YOU NEED TO KNOW?

Many newcomers to the EGE profession are overly concerned with how many exercises they want to learn. It is as if they think the more exercises they know the more they have to offer. Knowing lots of exercises is a false sense of security. In my experience one only needs a few of the most tried and true exercises to offer a comprehensive experience. I have experimented with many exercises I no longer teach or offer. I have seen other professionals offer booklets full of exercises that end up being gimmicky. The point is that the EGE professional should always know the purpose of the exercise.

In the EGE certification program I teach less than a dozen exercises. Each exercise can become ten or more exercises depending on the context I create for the activity. For example, the Observation exercise listed below can become an activity to allow your attention to wander wherever it wants to go. Or it can be an activity in exploring herd dynamics. Or it can be an exercise in exploring body language or non-verbal body language.

To make things more complicated, the EGE professional also needs to consider who the audience is and how they may respond individually and collectively. A simple observation exercise has different potential outcomes depending on if the audience is a group of adult leaders, youth at risk, veterans or housewives. In addition, the same exercise may influence individuals in a group very differently.

Add an additional wild card, the horse. So, you have a plan to offer a specific exercise to your audience, but then the horses are not going along with your plan. What do you do? An EGE professional needs to be trained well enough to know when they need to change their plan at any moment. Knowing what potential outcomes each exercise creates, allows the EGE professional to clearly direct the learning environment.

In the SkyHorseEGE™ certification program, we focus on training EGE professionals to know their teaching points and desired outcomes for every exercise and for their program as a whole. This knowledge allows them determine the appropriate exercises to offer to their specific audience at any given time.

Below are a few tried and true exercises and a summary of some of their potential goals and teaching points. Any of these exercises require extensive knowledge of horses.

Observation Exercise-Passive

This exercise if often done in the arena, but it can also be done in stalls or fields. Usually 1 to 4 horses are loose in the arena. They are free to go where they choose. Participants remain outside of the arena and observe the horses with a specific focus. Some potential explorations include noticing where your attention is drawn, what horse are you drawn to, how do you open your mind and move into an inquiry.

Herd Exercise-Passive

This exercise consists of several horses loose in an arena. It can also be done in a pasture environment where there are a herd of horses present. Participants are outside of the arena or pasture observing the horses. The EGE facilitator may offer various distinctions on herd dynamics, communication and coordination and then ask the participants to observe these distinctions within the horse herd, followed by conversations on how this may relate to their current life situations.

Round Pen –Passive or Active

A round pen experience is comprised of one horse in a round pen, a minimum of 50' in diameter, and one participant. This exercise is more challenging than the first two mentioned because the person is actually in the pen with a loose horse. The unpredictability of horses and their potentially aggressive responses must be considered and require that an EGE professional with excellent horsemanship skills be present at all times. Horses for this exercise need to have completed a rigorous interview process to determine their potential to become dangerous.

I do not advocate working the horse in an active exercise in the round pen. While some people train horses in round pens, I personally do not have EGE participants engage in actively moving the horse around the round pen. In passive round pen, the horses are allowed to come and go as they please.

Some topics that can be explored in the round pen include reflecting on a particular subject matter, developing a declaration, asking for intuitive insight and information, listening and developing relationships.

Leading In Hand-Active

The leading in hand exercise is always an active exercise. The horse is in a halter and lead rope and the goal is to have the participant lead the horse into a walk around the arena or a path. To make this exercise more potent, the EGE professional can guide the participant to make a specific declaration— declare a specific goal—that the walk will represent. The participant can also assign the horse a role. To do this the participant would answer the question, " Who does the horse represent for you on this walk?"

Some potential goals of this exercise include embodying your leadership goals, moving forward, creating a team, building trust, taking a stand and developing confidence.

Other exercises include lunging, team games, constellations, grooming, painting horses, drawing horses and much more. Most exercises can offer learning about relationships to self-others-world, confidence, telling your story, creating new paradigms, leadership, team dynamics, communication and coordination. The potential topics are far too numerous to go into detail at this time. Developing knowledge of horse behavior and psychology, human behavior and psychology, group dynamics and knowing one's teaching points are the first steps in creating an EGE environment.

Knowing Your Teaching Points

Before determining what exercises you plan to do, make sure that you have identified the core topics or themes you want to cover. What do you hope to accomplish? Are you in touch with the goals of your audience and do their match your intended goals?

In the initial phase of the EGE process, it is important to establish the reason you are going to engage in the EGE activity. If you are doing a private session, you most likely will begin by discussing the client's current topics and current emotional state before engaging with the horses. I usually do a thorough check-in before proceeding with horse activities, to get a sense of nuances that may need to be attended to with horses present.

If you are doing a group program, have all of your teaching points for each activity planned out ahead of time Try to set up your exercises and facilitate so that participants discover your teaching points on their own rather than you spending precious EGE time talking. Be prepared to re-iterate or point out your desired teaching points if the participants have not gotten them on their own. I usually have three to five teaching points I hope to reveal at my fingertips. I set up the exercise with a lot of open space for curiosity and discovery. I hope to see that the participant(s) are discovering my teaching points on their own. During the debrief I reinforce the teaching points as appropriate.

Below are some questions to help you prepare for an EGE session.

- What is the context (purpose) for my program?

- What is my context (purpose) for each exercise?

- How long do I plan to talk versus provide the experience itself?

- What are my teaching points?

- Do my teaching points reflect my overall promise?

- What does it mean to "hold the space of learning"?

- How do I plan to hold the space of learning?

- What phase of learning am I focusing on for each exercise?

MORE ON THE PROCESS OF FACILITATION

As mentioned earlier, your main role as a facilitator is to create a supportive learning environment for exploration, reflection, and integration of new insights and paradigms. Key competencies required include:

- Provide an open space for learning and change.

- Be able to identify the phases of change the participant is in and openness to learning.

- Encourage open exploration of core issues or breakdowns participant may be experiencing.

- Allow the possibility for long-lasting, sustainable change.

- Allow for a flexible agenda or plan of activities.

- Know when to enter into challenging areas and when to hold back.

- Attend to your own interpretations and how they may support client's insights and goals for change.

- Embody an open, grounded, inquisitive presence.

- Offer exercises or activities that are relevant to phase of change of client.

- Acknowledge intuitive and somatic perspectives versus an over-focus on mental interpretations (this is one of the truly unique features that having horses present in the change process offers).

- Know horse psychology and instinct.

- Respect the importance of body language (habits of physical presentation and its association with underlying moods and attitudes).

- Conduct ongoing appraisal of horse's response to participant(s).

- Maintain clear boundaries between being in horsemanship and EGE.

- Be able to ground your interpretations in somatic feedback including corresponding body posture, emotional resonance, mental interpretations, moods and attitudes, and how these relate to horse's responses.

- Encourage participants to discover their own insights.

- Assess participants' readiness to work with their issues.

- Allow time for the participants to be in their own breakdown or uncertainty. Do not rush to heal or fix.

- Offer grounded assessments as appropriate.

- Listen to, observe, and interpret the horse's response without judgment or your personal opinions.

- Avoid your own projections.

- Practice the art of asking open-ended questions.

- Ask questions that do not lead the client.

- Use open and curious inquiry versus direct probing.

- Ground your observations by connecting words and body signals with the actions of the horse.

- Do your assessments match the horse's response?

- Encourage participants to see things in a new light and look for possibility to reinterpret.

- Review patterns of thought, behavior, action, attitude.

- Look for opportunities to design new practices to promote integration of change.

YOUR PRACTICES DURING THE EGE PROCESS

Maintain an Open State of Mind

- Relax all of the muscles in your body.

- Soften your eyes and practice peripheral vision.

- Breathe into your belly, through your pelvis, and then into the ground.

- Notice your state of mind but do not fixate or attach.

- Notice how are you feeling.

- Notice your mood.

- Pay attention to your tone of voice.

- If you find yourself asking, "How am I doing?" you are not really attending to the participant. Refocus your attention on the participant and how he or she is doing.

- Make sure you are not energetically connected to the horse and thus distracting the horse from attending to the client. By this I mean, you do not want the horse to be attending to you. If the horse is connected to you too much, it will not be as interested in the participant.

Practice Open, Explorative Observation

- Take mental notes.

- Gather information.

- Avoid making rushed or quick conclusions.

Look For Patterns

- Notice patterns in thought, interpretations, words, actions, storyline.

- Notice words that pop out at you, such as luxury, always, hostile, and other unusual words.

- Identify non-verbal elements such as body language, body attitude, and mood of client that may correlate with words and thought.

- Does the participant trust you, your staff, and the horses?

- Is the participant's storyline repetitive or circular?

- Is there a particular tone of voice or change in body posture with certain words or storyline?

SUMMARY

- Know your underlying goals of an exercise and the specific actions to be practiced.

- Know your audience.

- Know what phase of change the participants are in.

- Be in the practices of EGE too.

Choosing Horses for EGE

I am looking for a horse that has a "kind eye." The horse has expression and life in its eyes. It is not dull or disengaged when I am around it. It is important to me that the horse shows some interest in me and in its surroundings, that it expresses an awareness and sensitivity to its environment. I do not want a horse that is flighty, spooky, or unsure of itself.

I want a horse that is interested in people and has a healthy sense of curiosity. And I want a horse that wants to do something, to be part of something, and that likes to work.

I want a horse that refers to me for direction when I am actively working with it. When the horse is unsure of what to do or how to respond, I want the horse to want to connect with me as opposed to disengaging and resorting to making its own decisions. This is very important. Part of this has to do with the horse's nature and part of it has to do with how I establish myself as the direction setter. Since I know that I have the competency to establish myself with the horse, I am looking primarily at the horse's nature in this case.

When I begin to work in hand with the horse, I am looking for a horse that wants to partner with me. One that wants to figure out what I am asking. I do not want a horse that becomes challenging, aggressive, or overly resistant. I also do not want a horse that is so passive that it just goes along with anything. I prefer a horse that knows itself and has its own sense of self-esteem.

As far as age of a horse, I do not have rules about the minimum age of a horse. I know that some associations have a standard rule about how old a horse should be to be working with the public.

EGE horses do not have to be rideable, since most, if not all, EGE work is done on the ground.

INTERVIEWING THE HORSE

Quiet yourself and allow yourself to enter into another state of consciousness. Walk around the arena for a few minutes to clear your head and sense the energy of the environment.

Make sure you are not in your head before you go to view the horses. If you have thoughts right away like, "I really like this horse," "She is so pretty," or "Oh, the poor horse looks unhappy," then you are still in your head and not listening with your more intuitive senses. Being in an intuitive state of consciousness does not have a lot of story to it. You may want to jot down notes so that your mind does not have to hold your thoughts.

Remember, you are not training the horse in this session. That is not your focus. Your focus is to listen and learn about the horse, not to fix the horse, work with issues that come up, or prove your prowess to the horse or to the human observers.

Step 1: Quiet Your Mind

- Do not focus on rational thoughts just yet.

- Feel your body temperature.

- Check that your muscles are relaxed.

- Feel the breeze, the quality of air and weather.

- Feel the ground; is it soft, warm, cool, or hard?

Step 2: Notice The Environment The Horse Is In

- Is the environment quiet?

- Where does the horse live?

- Does it get adequate exercise?

- What is the horse's diet? Is it on hot feed?

- What is the tone of the humans at the facility?

Step 3: Observe The Horse From A Distance

- Does the horse have a kind eye?

- Is its attitude openly expressed or is the horse dulled?

- Is the horse relaxed in its environment?

- Is the horse interested in the activities of the barn or is it recessed into the background, perhaps ignoring or avoiding contact?

- Is the horse's energy freely expressed or is it bunched up due to lack of movement or exercise or because it is over-confined?

Step 4: Approach The Horse In Its Stall Or Pasture

- How does the horse respond when you approach?

- Is it interested in you?

- Does it make contact right away or is it hesitant at first?

- Does it extend towards you in order to make contact?

- As you get closer, ask questions like, "Hey, who are you?" or "How are you? What's up?"

- Is the horse responsive and interested in you?

- As you reach out to touch the horse, what emotion does it express?

- What role does the horse play in the herd if it is in a pasture with other horses?

Step 5: Take The Horse Out Of Its Stall Or Pasture And Begin To Work In Hand

- How does the horse respond to pressure?

- Does the horse move easily off of subtle cues like breath, energy, and intention, or does it need tools to know what to do?

- If it is used to being tool or technique trained, you might take a bit of time here and see if it learns quickly to listen to your energy instead of its memorized cue-response.

- Apply a bit more pressure, or ask the horse with a bit more intensity so that you can see how it responds under pressure. Does it try to figure out what you want or does it resort to resistance right away?

- If you think the horse might tend to become resistant easily, you might be a little less refined in how you ask it to move so that you can see if it is patient or irritated under unusual pressure.

- Does the horse show any signs of aggression under pressure? If so, how extreme does it get?

There are many wild cards in EGE, and one of them is the unpredictability of horses. You may have a horse that you think does not have a mean bone in its body. It has always acted with calm and patience. The important question to answer is what will the horse do if it gets scared or anxious? How flighty will it become? How aggressively will it respond? Will it give you warning signs, or is its change in behavior dramatic and quick?

Horses can unexpectedly become dangerous in the EGE process when people in the program are being inauthentic or have unresolved trauma in their bodies. The horse sees the inauthenticity as a danger to their safety. It senses that the person is not telling the truth and should not be trusted. In this situation the horse will often become aggressive and either push into the person, bite or even kick at the person as if to say, "You are not trustworthy right now and therefore are unsafe to be around, so please get out of my space."

Horses can also become aggressive when a person in their proximity is experiencing extreme self-hate or self-judgment or judging you, but on the outside is pretending to be fine. For example, if somebody in the class doesn't really trust your facilitation or is overly self-conscious and feeling as if he or she is not part of the group, a horse may literally move that person out of the group.

During your interview with the horse you want to put the horse under unusual pressure because you want to see the range of aggression it may express. If a horse is quick to pin its ears back, nip, or threaten a kick, this behavior will only become more extreme in an EGE process. I would not use a horse that demonstrates such behavior while I am interviewing it.

Spookiness in a horse is also a factor to consider. All horses spook. The question is, how often does the horse spook, and when it does, how much of reaction does it embody? To me, it's not so important how often a horse spooks, it's what it does when it spooks. If, when a horse spooks, it does a 360 and an up-and-a-down and then takes off, or if it has no consideration of the people around it, it is not a safe EGE horse. I don't have spooky horses in my barn.

A horse that also won't work well in EGE is a horse that doesn't have good boundaries. A horse that has gotten away with pushing people or invading their space is going to have a field day in certain EGE sessions. Even the most well-trained and polite horse will begin to push on a person if that person has significant boundary issues.

Remember, the horse will mirror what the people in the environment are embodying. A person who has anger issues may bring out aggressive actions from your most gentle horse. A person who has boundary issues will stimulate your horse's hierarchal instincts, and an inauthentic person will bring out your horse's aggressiveness.

Some horses are not appropriate for passive activities where people are in the presence of loose horses. They may be very useful in leading-in-hand exercises, in which there is more structure around their role and expectations. Even just having them in a halter and lead rope will give you as the facilitator quite a bit more control. For some horses, having a halter and lead rope on makes them feel more comfortable as well, because it is more familiar to them.

Sometimes I recommend to people just starting out with EGE and still learning their horses' potential wild cards, to keep the horse in a halter and lead rope before having it loose with the public.

I also work very intuitively. If I have a sense that I can't really rely on a horse's behavior while I'm teaching or have my back turned, I might take that horse out of the process altogether. Some of my horses that I wouldn't put in a free space with people end up doing a lot of work with people over the fence. It always amazes me when a person with boundary issues manages to walk up to a fence with one of my more mouthy horses and end up with their jacket sleeve in the horse's mouth.

Just as with humans, there is a maturing process. Obviously, a one-year-old colt is going to have a lot more curiosity than a twenty-year-old mare and a much shorter attention span. There is also variance among breeds as well. Most horses mature with age. I have some horses who were too bold as younger horses, but after being around the EGE experience from the pasture and watching, they slowly learned how to relate to EGE.

Some horses make great leading in hand horses, while others are great in the round pen. Many horses may not be suited to all of the EGE activities. If in doubt, try the horse out in a grooming session first to see how it relates to the public and the EGE process.

Horse Handling During EGE Sessions

By Kansas Carradine, SkyHorseEGE™ Instructor

Those who venture to work with horses in a therapeutic context often do so in response to an innate desire to help, heal, or just to share the unique equine wisdom for the greater good of all. There is a strong passion to be of service in most all Equine Guided Educators, and while some may have ambitious goals for either successful financial or business return; very few enter into the field with aspirations of being performers in a "horse show." However, when working with horses in front of any audience, they become just that.

The thought of speaking publicly is enough to make many shy away from the facilitator role, but add horses to the situation, and the role becomes a whole different animal of unpredictability. While having our four-legged co-facilitators as part of the equation comforts many of us, there is still a lot to take into consideration when working with horses in front of individuals or large groups. Borrowing from my professional performance career in the equestrian world, I have outlined here some valuable tools that I would like to share in regards to working with horses while under public observation.

YOU ARE A ROLE MODEL

Public (adj.) - done, perceived, or existing in open view; of, concerning, or affecting the community or the people.

Being in the public eye means being assessed by others in regards to your competency and embodiment of the knowledge you are sharing. It means that what you offer as a service is leaving your domain and entering into the free-space, where it can be analyzed, appreciated, or discarded by anyone. They don't call it the public eye for nothing. We could actually refer to the public mind, which is far more subjective than the human eye (which is merely a lens or witness in the activity of observation), for it is the mind that captures a concept, processes it in accordance with the individual's belief system, and then categorizes that concept accordingly. Incidentally, when you are conducting an EGE program, all eyes will be on you and your every movement.

While not getting overly consumed by performance anxiety, I find it important not to diminish the agreement being made here. As an EGE professional, one commits to being a role model for others in the domains of horsemanship, presence, being open to the interpretations of others, and authenticity. Your audience will mimic and copy how you are with horses and the example you are setting for what you are asking them to study and practice. Therefore, it is important to know and study in yourself how you engage with horses from an EGE perspective.

MANAGING YOUR ENERGY

Being "on stage" with horses involves a virtual gymnastics of awareness exercises. It serves best to always monitor the energy of the group, the horses, the environment, and your own personal energy. In observing the client, the EGE facilitator is listening to the content of what is being said, the energy that is being communicated, as well as the somatics or body language being expressed. Reading the energy of the group and keeping a keen eye on the environment are more than enough to keep a person busy, but the most important aspect of the equation is YOU. Now, don't forget to attend to the horse.

As the horse handler, you must constantly remain in your own diligent practice of somatic awareness, not just when you are performing an exercise. Keep yourself balanced so that the energy can move through you freely and you become a good conduit for intuitive feedback. Watch your mental activity. If it becomes too laser like, that energy of fixation can influence the space. By the same principles, when the mind becomes too spread out, it can wander and lose focus. Remain soft and neutral with your mind, open to new possibilities or interpretations, and do a personal inventory to know where you are in relation to all things!

THE POWER OF NEUTRALITY

Throughout the course of a day, you will be inundated with a multitude of personal narratives, many of them having the power to evoke an emotional or critical response from your thinking mind. By staying in a neutral position, you free yourself up from the polarization of judgment. Jumping to conclusions and making fixed judgments can be not only emotionally and energetically draining for you, it can also create a less safe environment for your client if, in a moment, you become inauthentic to your horse. It is imperative that you keep an open heart and mind no matter the subject content. Your horse and client will thank you for it. How do you stay neutral? Through somatic awareness, relaxed breathing, and staying present.

KNOW YOUR AUDIENCE

One critical awareness is understanding the type of environment you are working in. Determining the kind of audience has a lot to do with how you handle your horse. If I am speaking to a group of horse people, of course, there is a certain level of energy that is more relaxed, and you can understand that people know and have experience in responding to horse behavior or tuning it out when it is not the focal point of conversation. That is to say, if you have a group of office employees or city folks who have no experience with animals or horses, you are also more careful to minimize the movements and interactions of both you and the horse because they will become very captivating.

The way I handle a horse for one of Ariana's corporate groups in a one-day session is in sharp contrast with the way I would conduct myself on day three of an EGE-1 workshop where trust has been built and so much context and experience have been acquired.

BE PROFESSIONAL

We all know how it feels to be relaxed around our own horses, to joke with them, play around with them, hang on them, and embrace the overall levity horses can bring into our daily life. Presenting Equine Guided Education in the business format, however, demands professionalism. Having a professional attitude will aid in the client's developing clear confidence in you as a facilitator.

As a young girl growing up on a ranch, I knew that there were times to laugh and play around, but we all knew the difference between show-time and barn time. Remember, people will be quicker to judge and criticize what they don't understand. You have a wonderful opportunity to give EGE a good name for those who are either unfamiliar or skeptical. Even more so, seasoned horse professionals are going to keep a close eye on how you handle the horses because it is in their range of knowledge, just as a pilot will always notice the landing of any plane that touches ground. He is intimately connected to the ins and outs of flying a plane; so too should you always be making a point to stay connected with the horsemanship tools and philosophies you are modeling.

PRACTICE GOOD HORSEMANSHIP

No matter what your level your horsemanship, there is always room to grow. I say this because even though I may be an expert in one field of equestrian arts, I am a beginner in at least a dozen others. The horse world is vast. There is no limit to how far our knowledge can extend. Improving your skill with horses is as important to your business as maintaining the horse's physical health. If there is something that comes up with your horse, get help and guidance from a trusted trainer that knows more than you. Be willing to learn in every situation from both your horse and others who have accumulated experience. There is nothing that can substitute for "miles in the saddle." What you will learn from a horse on a daily ride is just as relevant to what happens in the EGE context. Having a strong foundation in horsemanship will give you the confidence to believe in yourself and your practices, and your clients and horses will find security in that attitude of stability.

It is important to keep in mind that anytime you are accepting the help of another, you must still listen to your inner guidance. Listen to your intuition and don't be afraid to make a change if the other person's methods do not suit your horse.

REMAIN CONSISTENT

Remain consistent in all of your horsemanship practices; even the smallest detail is important. Keeping your barn in order, and always having tack in the same place, develops a unity and order that translates to all areas of the work. Tie a horse to the same place, and practice the same principles in your barn whether you are alone or with others. In a world where ritual has largely given way to routine, the activity of taking out the horse, tying her up, and brushing her is very therapeutic for both horse and rider.

There is actually a huge potential for EGE growth points here. When you establish the ritual with clients or riders, how do they identify with that? Is there a need for ritual in their own lives? How do they feel when things are "out of sync"? It can be a good study for noticing attachments as well, such as being attached to the outcome of how something is "supposed to work out."

When you catch a horse, do it the same way every time. Imagine that your clients are observing you. Ask yourself how you want to embody your relationship with the horse and what you would want to teach during an EGE session. Turn your horse back out in the field with the same awareness and repetition. This is helpful because it will create a standard that you can rely on. This shows respect and awareness for both the horse and for the task at hand. Be aware of how the horse is feeling as you approach, of how you put the halter on, fastening all buckles completely, and carrying the lead rope neatly. Remember, everyone is watching, so you have to model it well.

DO NOT OVERLY BOND WITH THE HORSE

Sometimes it is hard to resist, but when presenting in front of the public, it's important to refrain from getting all lovey-dovey with your horses. It is fine to appreciate them, wonderful in fact to feel and express heartfelt gratitude for their contribution. However, when we overly indulge in cuddle-type behavior, it can detract from the client's experience and it can also stimulate behavior in the horse that is undesirable. If, for example, I make a point of vigorously rubbing my horse each time it approaches, I am setting up a precedent that might not be appropriate at all times.

Picture this: You walk toward a lover or a horse with eyes locked, swimming in the nostalgia of intimacy and affection. Your body is open and you feel warmth in your chest and torso as you approach. Upon reaching each other, you shower the additional affection of a loving embrace and stroking hands.

Another scenario: You enter a meeting or classroom for study, where others are already seated. You are aware of yourself as you approach another, keeping your energy soft, but drawn in so as not to disturb the equilibrium of the group.

It is easy to see here the contrast between these two interactions and how we can choose to carry our energy. In the first, you are really drawing in a person's energy and allowing it to envelop you. In the second, you are aware of your own personal energy and not overly trying to pull attention away from anyone in the space. Every facilitator will benefit from the awareness of how he or she chooses to direct energy in any given moment.

There is a difference between *making a connection* and having a *working relationship*. When you are working with your horse, it has a job to do, and that job requires the horse's attention to the client. If you remove yourself as an obstacle to the horse's concentration, then there is a clear conduit for information to flow. When you remain as a strong influence in their field, there is static, so to speak, on the line. Retain a professional distance by clearly designating "work behavior" and being consistent in the way you handle yourself in client sessions.

USE DISCERNMENT

Proper discernment is an art form. It involves timing, wisdom, finesse, feeling, and ultimately is guided by the intuitive force of knowing when to say what. In the right moment, just a few words can mean so much, and at the same time, too many can extinguish the spark of a new insight. In the course of any session, there will be obvious times for feedback, as well as the more subtle occasions when feedback needs to be gentle or specific, direct or compassionate. When in doubt, ask for inner guidance, or just follow the lead of the horse and share silence. Less is more. Often, when a client is processing something, we do not need to draw attention to every action, even if the horse is continuing to respond. (Unless, of course, a horse is mirroring something over and over again. Then, we know that a message needs to be communicated.) Quietly holding the space is a powerful tool that builds richness.

BE SUBTLE

When making adjustments to a horse's position, or when setting up for a new exercise, be mindful of how you can facilitate blending your energy into the herd, and make corrections as smoothly as possible. It is with artful grace that we move slowly and quietly among the horses without disruption, taking our clear role as sculptor of the arena dynamic when we need to make a change, be it removing a horse or removing a potential hazard. Be on "horse-time" and move more slowly than you usually do, as this practice can quiet the mind as well as the herd.

The Power of Being a Student

By Hallie Bigliardi, SkyHorseEGE™ Instructor

Since 2010, I have had the opportunity to work with Ariana at SkyHorseEGE™ for dozens of EGE certification courses and numerous other public and private programs. I have witnessed hundreds of people from around the world come to learn from Ariana how to incorporate Equine guided Education into their professional offerings. This particular demographic of students is often different than others who come strictly for their own self-development.

I remember Ariana often saying how the certification program can be more difficult to teach because there are a lot of unconscious expectations of students that don't exist in other public programs. She would often remember the same unique dynamics appearing in the Somatic Coaching Program she co-developed for Strozzi Institute, which was also a certification program.

In the paragraphs that follow, I will offer some suggestions about how to get the most out of the SkyHorseEGE™ certification program. I will share the benefits of continuing education and the unique learning that comes from returning to the SkyHorseEGE™ certification program as an advanced student. I will also share my discovery of EGE as a way of being, not just at the stable, but also in all areas of life. The SkyHorseEGE™ certification offers the best training for people who want to incorporate horses into their professional offer, but it is so much more! This program can benefit people from all walks of life by teaching them how to better communicate and how to improve their connection to themselves, others and the greater whole (nature, earth, cosmos, etc.).

At its heart, EGE is not just about a specific process of horse-human interaction. It is not about a list of exercises and activities. All of these things help to create the space for learning, so we can open ourselves up to what wants to come to form and to the underlying messages that want to be heard.

While many programs and processes are designed to help us qualify, quantify, and zero in on THE answer, EGE encourages us to discover, gain new insights and new solutions through intuitive, non-linear processes. This type of learning can be more challenging because we are trained to emphasize our rational thought process to formulate and create. A major component of EGE process is to literally let go of what we know and be in an open curiosity without actually looking for the answers. This takes practice because the educational systems we are raised in train us to quantify, qualify, categorize, compartmentalize, and get the solutions as quickly as possible.

This can be challenging for EGE certification students because they have an underlying desire to look good, do it right, and show their expertise and knowledge. Sometimes it takes awhile to realize that the best way to learn is to *be the student*. Be curious, ask questions. Avoid spending a lot of time talking about what you already know. Allow yourself to explore lots of different styles, options, and opinions. Ariana often reminds students that sometimes it is just as important to know what you don't want to do, as it is to know how you want to do it.

The first phase of EGE is about experimenting within a specific inquiry. By creating a space of possibility, students explore different thoughts and ideas. Sometimes it takes time to allow our "other" senses to inform our inquiry. Most of us have trained our logical mind to discount or over-rule our intuitive and sensate feelings and impressions, even though we may believe that we are quite intuitive.

The SkyHorseEGE™ process is unlike other learning models that take place in a classroom or conference room. Because horses naturally cut right to the core of a person's inner dynamics, the SkyHorseEGE™ certification program can get quite personal. Sometimes EGE students feel an increased sense of vulnerability. Their quiet reflection might go something like this, "I came here to learn EGE, not to do my own work." The funny thing is, the only way to really learn EGE is to do it. It is definitely a *learning by doing* process. There is no way a person could learn how to do this kind of work by reading about it or listening to lectures. It must be viscerally, visually, kinesthetically, and sensately experienced. The good news here is that having gone through it wholeheartedly allows to the practitioner to come from a grounded place of experience. Going through the process that they will later be guiding others through is an important element. I have witnessed a few students who did not want to be learners. They just wanted to get the information and exercises and the stamp of approval. Problem is, it is hard to coach other people if they themselves are not coachable.

For most students there is a natural desire to show competency and assimilation of the concepts and principles. Yet, because of the horse's ability to sniff out authentic versus inauthentic participation, at some point in the program, there is tension between this feeling of vulnerability and the desire to demonstrate competency and receive approval. EGE requires a deep level of openness and surrender. Those that are able to embrace their vulnerability and really put themselves into the EGE process are able to make huge strides in their development on both a personal and professional level. It is through immersing oneself into the EGE process that one actually gains competency and experience of EGE.

By embracing our own vulnerability, we make it okay for others to do the same, and we develop the level of trust required to facilitate the EGE work. To be successful at EGE, one must be able to trust the horse, trust oneself, trust the process, and build trust with the participants. Tolerating the discomfort of vulnerability is essential. No one can embody the work unless he or she has let it into their core, and participants will not follow or fully put their trust in a facilitator if that facilitator has not done his or her own work.

Think of developing this skill of vulnerability as you think of developing the skill of flexibility. How an EGE session unfolds, where it is going to take us, is always a big unknown. A key component of facilitating EGE process is to follow the horse, and follow the non-linear flow of information. The ability to facilitate EGE comes through the willingness to allow this feeling of vulnerability and re-interpret its quality as a natural part of the learning process and not something to be avoided.

Linda Kohanov also talks about vulnerability in her book, *The Power of the Herd*. In her Emotional Message Chart, she lists the message of the emotion of vulnerability as this: "Something significant is about to change or be revealed (internal threat to self-image, beliefs, comfortable habits)." The other definitions I came across implied openness or exposure to potential danger or harm, which implies that the thing we are exposed to is "negative" or harmful. However, in the EGE process, whether it is a gift or talent or a disempowering belief or habit that is being brought to light, the impending revelation or change comes with a positive potential, presenting us with an opportunity to move forward and away from something that is harmful or holding us back.

To embrace this vulnerability, requires "letting go" - letting go of what we think we know, letting go of our "plan," letting go of the need to be "right," and tuning into what "is" and what the horses are reflecting. As facilitators, we enter this state every time we engage in the EGE process with a participant or group. The magic happens when we truly trust the process and the feeling of vulnerability actually transforms into a feeling of freedom. For me now as a SkyHorseEGE™ Instructor of EGE, this is one of my most trusted tools – trusting the horses and that the process that needs to unfold will do so if I don't fixate on my agenda for the day.

I know the importance of embracing the unknown with curiosity and openness. The only way to develop the level of trust and hone the skills required for EGE is to be in the practice of EGE – doing the work itself and returning to the learning environment to experience the uniqueness each group creates in their program. The Equine Guided Educators who return to SkyHorseEGE™ as advanced students develop EGE skills dramatically faster than those who do not. Not every student can return since some live far, far away. But again, my experience is that those who stay connected even through coaching and mentoring are able to integrate EGE into their professional offerings faster. I also know that some people need to take their time and move at their own pace of development.

During the EGE certification program (or any self-development/learning program), there is only so much we can absorb. It can take time for what we learn to settle in and become embodied. Each time I returned to a new SkyHorseEGE™ program, I was able to experience the concepts and principles from a different perspective. I was able to recognize the principles I already had, and absorb some of the deeper concepts I did not have the capacity to see or understand during my previous experience. I found myself in different conversations and processes than I experienced the first (second, third . . . or seventh) time through. Each time I was able to track more of what was happening within myself and the group. There is always more to learn, and the deep levels we go to during the certification program provide the greatest opportunity to exponentially increase your learning and development. Even Ariana still says that she is always learning something new during the EGE programs.

After I completed my certification program in 2010, I thought the way my class went was THE WAY it was done. I was fortunate to be in a class where everyone was very engaged and willing to work hard and go all in. We challenged each other, encouraged each other, and held a high expectation for ourselves as individuals and as a group. In talking with fellow CEGE from other classes, I noticed they, too, thought that the way their certification programs happened was "THE WAY" they always happen. However, after having been a staff member in multiple EGE-1 and EGE-2 programs, I discovered that no two SkyHorseEGE™ programs are ever the same. There are a variety of choice points that present with different groups. Of course, the core teaching points and concepts are covered in every class, but the order in which they are presented varies. Different themes emerge with each class, so additional teaching points are brought in and more time is spent on certain topics or exercises to address the specific themes.

Students who return to SkyHorseEGE™ gain a whole new perspective on how the EGE exercises can be set up in so many different ways as well as a deeper understanding of how to follow the horses, follow the energy, and the true meaning of *trusting the process*. By far the greatest benefit to returning to SkyHorseEGE™ is to study and practice with Ariana. I am continually inspired by the mastery with which she is able to track each student, to recognize and later recall students' somatic patterns, and to hold the space for all of them. Certified SkyHorseEGE™ who return are encouraged to participate in the program from a different perspective as advanced students. As students develop a deeper understanding of the core concepts and principles, they can turn their inquiry to imagining they were actually teaching the EGE process. The inquiry goes something like this: "If I were facilitating, what would I say or do?" This practice has really helped me hone my skills as a facilitator and teacher.

SkyHorseEGE™ certification program offers some of the best coach and facilitation training available, and in my opinion, its benefit to non-equine practitioners is underestimated. The EGE process trains the skills of observation and communication unlike any other program I am aware of, whether or not one plans to incorporate horses into one's professional offerings. In fact, with an intense focus on intuition, awareness, non-verbal communication, openness, curiosity, and non-judgment, EGE is also "a way of being," not merely a self-development or learning process. It is a way of being in the world, a set of practices for listening and communicating. Continuing to study EGE has not only increased my skills as a coach and facilitator, but it has improved my way of being in all areas of my life.

Life is really about our relationships and in the SkyHorseEGE™ programs everything we study and teach has to do with how we are relating to ourselves, how we are relating to others, and how we are relating to our worldview. All of the tools and exercises are intended to bring us into a more authentic presence that is focused on what we care about. So whether you are looking to incorporate horses into your professional offerings, enhance your existing coaching, teaching, and facilitation skills, or simply want to be more of who you are in all areas of your life, I can tell you from my own personal experience, the horses and the SkyHorseEGE™ programs will help you get there.

Conclusion

I hope this book has offered you some tools to practice and develop your skill as an Equine Guided Educator. May you always remember to be a student of life. May the field of Equine Guided Education prosper and contribute to people wherever, whenever, for the sake of healing our relations within ourselves, within our communities, and within our most sacred connection to our Great Mother.

Remember to stay on the path of exploration and inquiry as if you were discovering the hidden gifts of nature for the first time. Revel in the wisdom that comes before thought, the wisdom that is felt rather than thoughtfully rationalized. Now is a time to design new paradigms for how we think, how we learn and how we live. Stay on the path. Don't worry about the final destination. You don't need to know each step of the way. There is no instruction manual for your life. If you follow your heart authentically and courageously, your destiny will find you.

Bibliography

Abrams, David. *Spell of the Sensuous*. NY: Pantheon Books, 1996.

Arrien, Angeles. *The Fourfold Way, Walking the Paths of the Warrior, Teacher, Healer, and Visionary*. San Francisco: Harper, 1993.

Armstrong, Thomas. *Seven Kinds of Smart*. New York: Plume/Penguin, 1993.

Bennett-Goleman, Tara. *Emotional Alchemy*. New York: Harmony Books, 2001.

Budiansky, Stephen. *The Nature of Horses*. New York: The Free Press, 1997.

Curtis, Helena. *Biology*. New York: Worth Publishers, 1979.

Deloria Jr., Vine, and Wildcat, Daniel R. *Power and Place: Indian Education in America*. Colorado: Fulcrum Resources, 2001.

Diamond, Jared. *Guns, Germs and Steel*. New York: W.W. Norton & Co., 1999.

Gatto, John Taylor. *A Different Kind of Teacher*.

Grandin, Temple, and Johnson, Catherine. *Animals in Translation*. New York: Scribner, 2005.

Horowitz, Mardi J. *Cognitive Psychodynamics*. Canada: John Wiley & Sons, 1998.

Horowitz, Mardi J. *Formulation, as a Basis for Planning Psychotherapy Treatment*. Wash. DC: American Psychiatric Press, Inc., 1997.

Kohanov, Linda. *The Tao of Equus*. Novato: New World Library, 2001.

Leider, Richard J., and Shapiro, David A. *Repacking Your Bags*. San Francisco, Berrett Koehler, 2002.

Swift, Sally. *Centered Riding*. Vermont: A Trafalgar Square Farm Book, 1985.

About the Author

Ariana Strozzi Mazzucchi is an internationally recognized pioneer in Equine Guided Education field, beginning EGE in the late 1980's and coining the term, "Equine Guided Education in the late 1990's. She is a lifelong horsewoman, master somatic coach, zoologist, and entrepreneur. Among her many accomplishments, Ariana co founded Strozzi Institute, the Center for Leadership and Mastery, SkyHorseEGE™ (formerly known as SkyHorse Ranch), and recently renamed the ranch Casari Ranch.

With innovative vision, Ariana blended her knowledge of animal biology, business process, somatics, and human development into an experiential format guided by horses. She realized quickly that horses could reveal the human's developmental process much quicker and with much more profound results than any other self-development, coaching, or therapy program she had ever witnessed.

As she developed Equine Guided Education, she also realized that nature, land, and the wonders of the local geography itself play an instrumental and unique role in helping people get in touch with who they are and what they care about. In some way, this was no surprise to Ariana, as she grew up in the coastal headlands rich in wildness, beauty, frankness, honesty, and inspiration. What she had not expected was that all people could benefit from time in nature and experiences with horses present.

Nature and animals do not live in the language of the rational mind. They live in the *essence* of communication made up of non-verbal cues, body language, emotional intelligence, feeling, and instinct. Ariana has been familiar with that language since childhood, having lived with dyslexia, often finding the natural world to be her healing place.

A California native, Ariana began her horsemanship career at the age of 7. As her talent and versatility with horses was quickly recognized, she won many championship awards in the disciplines of eventing, dressage, jumping, reining, working cowhorse, and gymkhana. She began working for a variety of horse ranches starting at the age of 9 and has been working with horses ever since.

Ariana supported herself through college by training horses and graduated from U.C. Davis in 1984 specializing in animal behavior and wildlife ecology. In addition to her work with horses, she spent many years healing wild animals, zoo animals and domestic pets. Ariana innovated the use of physical therapy into the rehabilitation of birds of prey at the U.C. Davis Raptor Center. After she presented the use of physical therapy on wild animals at several national conferences, the use of physical therapy is now utilized in raptor centers throughout the United States.

Her wild patients and the birds of prey taught her the same principles as the horses, the very principles that this book is based upon.

Ariana began studying leadership in the mid 1980s, when she began putting together the pieces that were to become what we now know as Equine Guided Education. Since that time she has created many businesses that prosper to this day. She has served on many boards, and is on the faculty of Institute for Women's Leadership, Institute for Generative Leadership, and Meridian University. Her corporate clients include U.C. Berkeley Haas School of Business Development, Institute of Noetic Sciences, Facebook, Kaiser, Pfizer, Nike, Genentech, Visa Credit Card, Wells Fargo Bank, Proctor & Gamble, Hewlett-Packard, Cisco, Apple Inc., Leadership USA, PSI Seminars, Newfield Network, and Trainer Communications.

In addition to her public service, Ariana has worked with thousands of individuals and has been teaching people how to incorporate horses into their professional offerings since the late 1990s.

Her other books include, *Horse Sense for the Leader Within*, *Planning Your Business in the Horse as Healer/Teacher Professions*, and the video, *Intuitive Horsemanship™* in addition to numerous essays in other books and publications. She lives and works on a 530-acre sheep and horse ranch along the Northern California coast with her family.

Made in the USA
Middletown, DE
26 September 2023

39341228R00142